Jello Salads 250

(Jello Salads - Volume 1)

Enjoy 250 Days with Amazing Jello Salad Recipes in Your Own Jello Salad Cookbook!

Henry Fox

Contents

Introduction

***

Food can be good or bad—that's a well-known fact. This cookbook "Jello Salads 250 Volume 1" explores a variety of ideas for unique, healthy, and easy-to-make Jello Salads. The distinct blend of ingredients results not only in rich flavors but also plenty of nutrients for good health. All those protein, vitamins, fiber, and other nutrients help regulate metabolism as well as relieve stress and other elements that harm the body. The hardest part of putting this book together is demystifying some of the popular myths about food. Case in point: shrimp and eggs that are high in cholesterol, yet they don't affect the blood's cholesterol level. In addition, shrimp and eggs are necessary foods for a balanced diet. Another food misconception I want to debunk is the use of fat-free food that started centuries ago. Although it is a must to avoid fat for meat-based dishes, it hardly makes sense in salads. It's because the fats and oils in many salad dressings help the body absorb more fat-soluble vitamins (A, D, E, and K) found in fresh veggies. Seeds and nuts help in reducing weight, too. Isn't that great?

My wonderful husband and two children inspired me to produce this book. As a personal wellness and nutrition consultant, I traveled to Ukraine and Western Russia, the Caucasus, and Eastern Europe. Being a professional food specialist, I began to eagerly gather nuggets of cooking wisdom, examine them, and use them with success. After tying the knot, I began to serve various healthy and delicious meals to my family at the dining table. No harm has been done to their health! So now, I'm sharing my experience with you, beginning with Jello Salad Recipes. Here's hoping the recipes would inspire you to become healthier!

You also see more different types of salad recipes

such as:

- ✓ *Diabetic Salads*
- ✓ *Grain Salads*
- ✓ *Salads for Two*
- ✓ *Turkey Salads*
- ✓ *Coleslaw*
- ✓ *...*

Thank you for choosing "Jello Salads 250 Volume 1". I really hope that each book in the series will be always your best friend in your little kitchen.

Let's live happily and eat more Jello Salads every day!

Enjoy the book,

250 Amazing Jello Salads Recipes

***

- Fiber: 0 g

1. 7 Layer Gelatin Salad

Here's an eye-catching salad that my mother makes for Christmas dinner each year. You can choose different flavors to make other color combinations for specific holidays or other gatherings. --Jan Hemness, Stockton, Missouri

Serving: 20 servings. | Prep: 30 m | Cook: 0 m | Ready in: 30 m

Ingredients

- 4-1/2 cups boiling water, divided
- 7 packages (3 ounces each) assorted flavored gelatin
- 4-1/2 cups cold water, divided
- 1 can (12 ounces) evaporated milk, divided
- 1 carton (8 ounces) frozen whipped topping, thawed
- Sliced strawberries and kiwifruit, optional

Direction

- In a small bowl, add 3/4 cup boiling water to one gelatin package; stir 2 minutes to completely dissolve. Stir in 3/4 cup cold water. Pour into a 3-qt. trifle or glass bowl. Refrigerate until set but not firm, about 40 minutes.
- In a clean bowl, dissolve another gelatin package into 1/2 cup boiling water. Stir in 1/2 cup cold water and 1/2 cup milk. Spoon over the first layer. Refrigerate until set but not firm.
- Repeat five times, alternating plain and creamy gelatin layers. Refrigerate each layer until set but not firm before adding the next layer. Refrigerate, covered, overnight. Serve with whipped topping and, if desired, fruit.

Nutrition Information

- Calories: 163 calories
- Total Fat: 3g
- Cholesterol: 6mg
- Sodium: 85mg
- Total Carbohydrate: 30g
- Protein: 4g

2. Anglers Gelatin Delight

Get in the swim with this refreshing cucumber-lime molded salad, a hit at my theme party! Any fish or shell-shaped mold would work well for this salad, but if you don't have one, you can improvise with common pan shapes as shown. --Martha Conaway, Pataskala, Ohio

Serving: 6 servings. | Prep: 15 m | Cook: 0 m | Ready in: 15 m

Ingredients

- 1 medium cucumber, peeled
- 1 package (3 ounces) lime gelatin
- 1 cup boiling water
- 1 cup chopped celery
- 1 small onion, chopped
- 1 cup (8 ounces) 4% cottage cheese
- 3/4 cup mayonnaise
- 1 tablespoon lemon juice
- 1 raisin
- 1 sweet red pepper strip
- Lemon and lime slices, green grapes and celery leaves, optional

Direction

- Cut one slice from center of cucumber for fish's eye; chill. Peel and chop remaining cucumber. In a large bowl, dissolve gelatin in water. Add the celery, onion and chopped cucumber. Stir in the cottage cheese, mayonnaise and lemon juice. Pour into one 8-in. round pan and one 8-in. square pan (or a 6-cup fish and lobster mold) coated with cooking spray. Refrigerate overnight or until set.
- Unmold round pan onto a 14-in. round serving platter. Unmold square pan onto a cutting board; cut in half diagonally to form two triangles. Position one triangle on the platter so tip touches circle, forming the tail. Cut remaining triangle in half. Place one half

on top of the circle and the other on the bottom for fins; gently curve fins toward the tail.

- For the eye, place reserved cucumber slice on the side of the circle opposite the tail; place raisin in center. Add red pepper strip for mouth. Garnish with lemon and lime slices, grapes and celery leaves if desired. Chill until serving.

Nutrition Information

- Calories: 307 calories
- Total Fat: 24g
- Cholesterol: 18mg
- Sodium: 333mg
- Total Carbohydrate: 17g
- Protein: 6g
- Fiber: 1g

3. Apple Cherry Salad

"Our family enjoys this refreshing salad with its different textures and crunch. The economical recipe is my mother's," says Karen Harrington of Le Mars, Iowa.

Serving: 8-10 servings. | Prep: 20 m | Cook: 0 m | Ready in: 20 m

Ingredients

- 1 package (3 ounces) cherry gelatin
- 1 cup boiling water
- 1 can (21 ounces) cherry pie filling
- 4 medium apples, chopped
- 1 cup chopped celery

Direction

- In a large bowl, dissolve gelatin in boiling water. Stir in the pie filling, apples and celery. Refrigerate for 30 minutes or until chilled.

Nutrition Information

- Calories: 134 calories
- Total Fat: 0 g

- Cholesterol: 0 mg
- Sodium: 40mg
- Total Carbohydrate: 33g
- Protein: 1g
- Fiber: 2g

4. Apple Cider Gelatin Salad

Apple cider and crisp apples lend a hint of fall to this refreshing salad that's perfect for autumn and holiday gatherings. A dear neighbor lady shared the recipe with me.
-Cyndi Brinkhaus, South Coast Metro, California

Serving: 6 servings. | Prep: 20 m | Cook: 0 m | Ready in: 20 m

Ingredients

- 2 envelopes unflavored gelatin
- 1/2 cup cold water
- 2 cups apple cider or juice
- 1/2 cup sugar
- 1/3 cup lemon juice
- 1/4 teaspoon ground cloves
- Dash salt
- 1 cup diced unpeeled apples
- 1/2 cup chopped walnuts
- 1/2 cup chopped celery
- TOPPING:
- 3/4 cup sour cream
- 1/4 cup mayonnaise
- 1 tablespoon sugar
- Ground cinnamon
- Cinnamon sticks, optional

Direction

- In a small bowl, sprinkle gelatin over cold water; let stand for 1 minute.
- In a large saucepan, bring cider to a boil; stir in the gelatin mixture and sugar until dissolved. Stir in lemon juice, cloves and salt. Pour into a large bowl. Refrigerate until slightly thickened, about 1 hour.
- Fold in apples, walnuts and celery. Pour into a 1-qt.dish or individual dishes. Refrigerate until firm, about 2 hours.

- For topping, in a small bowl, combine the sour cream, mayonnaise and sugar until blended. Dollop over salad; sprinkle with cinnamon. Serve with cinnamon sticks if desired.

Nutrition Information

- Calories: 328 calories
- Total Fat: 18g
- Cholesterol: 23mg
- Sodium: 112mg
- Total Carbohydrate: 36g
- Protein: 6g
- Fiber: 1g

---

5. Apple Cider Salad

I especially like to present this salad at holiday potlucks. By adding food coloring to the bottom layer, I can easily create a fun, festive look.

Serving: 6-8 servings. | Prep: 25 m | Cook: 0 m | Ready in: 25 m

Ingredients

- 1-3/4 cups apple cider or juice, divided
- 1 package (3 ounces) cherry gelatin
- 1 cup chopped peeled apple
- 1 envelope unflavored gelatin
- 1/4 cup cold water
- 1 cup applesauce
- 3 ounces cream cheese, softened
- 1 can (5 ounces) evaporated milk
- Red or green food coloring, optional

Direction

- In a small saucepan, bring 1 cup apple cider to a boil. Remove from the heat; stir in cherry gelatin until dissolved. Stir in remaining cider. Chill until mixture begins to thicken. Stir in apples. Pour into an oiled 6-cup mold; chill until set.
- Meanwhile, soften unflavored gelatin in cold water. In a saucepan, whisk applesauce and cream cheese until smooth. Add milk and

unflavored gelatin; cook and stir over low heat for 4 minutes or until gelatin completely dissolves. Add food coloring if desired.
- Chill until mixture begins to thicken. Pour over first layer. Chill until set. Unmold onto a serving platter.

Nutrition Information

- Calories: 148 calories
- Total Fat: 5g
- Cholesterol: 17mg
- Sodium: 80mg
- Total Carbohydrate: 23g
- Protein: 4g
- Fiber: 1g

---

6. Apple Cranberry Delight

"My husband and I went to a cranberry festival, and I came home with 5 pounds of the berries! Luckily they freeze well and taste great in this simple dish that I use in place of fruit." Beverly Koester - Appleton, Wisconsin

Serving: 6 servings. | Prep: 20 m | Cook: 5 m | Ready in: 25 m

Ingredients

- 1-1/2 cups fresh or frozen cranberries
- 1-3/4 cups unsweetened apple juice, divided
- 1 package (.3 ounce) sugar-free cranberry gelatin
- 2 cups chopped peeled Golden Delicious apples

Direction

- In a small saucepan, combine cranberries and 1 cup apple juice. Bring to a boil. Reduce heat; cover and simmer for 10-15 minutes or until the berries pop. Stir in gelatin until dissolved. Remove from the heat; stir in apples and remaining apple juice.
- Pour into a 4-cup mold coated with cooking spray. Refrigerate for 4 hours or until firm. Unmold onto a serving plate.

Nutrition Information

- Calories: 70 calories
- Total Fat: 0 g
- Cholesterol: 0 mg
- Sodium: 42mg
- Total Carbohydrate: 16g
- Protein: 1g
- Fiber: 2g

7. AppleCinnamon Gelatin

This ruby-red gelatin is a festive addition to your holiday spread. Cinnamon red-hot candies add a unique flavor.-- Suzy Horvath, Gladstone, Oregon

Serving: 8 servings. | Prep: 30 m | Cook: 0 m | Ready in: 30 m

Ingredients

- 2 packages (3 ounces each) cranberry gelatin
- 1-1/2 cups water
- 3 tablespoons red-hot candies
- 1-1/2 cups cold water
- 2 medium tart apples, peeled and chopped
- 1 package (8 ounces) cream cheese, softened

Direction

- Place gelatin in a large bowl. In a small saucepan, combine water and candies. Cook and stir until candies are dissolved and mixture comes to a boil. Stir into gelatin. Stir in cold water.
- Set aside 1 cup gelatin mixture; let stand at room temperature. Refrigerate remaining gelatin until set but not firm. Fold in apples; pour into a 6-cup mold coated with cooking spray. Refrigerate for 30 minutes or until firm.
- In a small bowl, beat cream cheese until smooth. Gradually beat in reserved gelatin; carefully spoon over apple layer. Cover and refrigerate for at least 6 hours. Unmold onto a serving platter.

Nutrition Information

- Calories: 212 calories
- Total Fat: 10g
- Cholesterol: 31mg
- Sodium: 132mg
- Total Carbohydrate: 28g
- Protein: 4g
- Fiber: 1g

8. Applesauce Gelatin Squares

"I make this attractive soft-set salad during the holidays and garnish it with ranch dressing that's tinted green," relates Judy Ernst of Montague, Michigan. "Or spoon on a dollop of whipped topping for a light sweet dessert anytime."

Serving: 16 servings. | Prep: 5 m | Cook: 0 m | Ready in: 5 m

Ingredients

- 4 packages (.3 ounce each) sugar-free raspberry gelatin or flavor of your choice
- 4 cups boiling water
- 2 cups cold water
- 1 jar (46 ounces) unsweetened applesauce

Direction

- In a bowl, dissolve gelatin in boiling water. Stir in cold water and applesauce. Pour into a 13-in. x 9-in. dish coated with cooking spray. Refrigerate for 8 hours or overnight. Cut into squares.

Nutrition Information

- Calories: 42 calories
- Total Fat: 0 g
- Cholesterol: 0 mg
- Sodium: 48mg
- Total Carbohydrate: 10g
- Protein: 1g
- Fiber: 0 g

9. ApplesauceBerry Gelatin Mold

Want a head start on your holiday meal? Try this uncomplicated, yet pretty apple-berry mold from Gloria Coates of Madison, Connecticut. Fresh cranberries and mint leaves are a beautiful garnish.

Serving: 12 servings. | Prep: 10 m | Cook: 0 m | Ready in: 10 m

Ingredients

- 2 packages (3 ounces each) strawberry gelatin
- 2 cups boiling water
- 1 can (14 ounces) whole-berry cranberry sauce
- 1-3/4 cups chunky applesauce

Direction

- In a large bowl, dissolve gelatin in boiling water. Stir in cranberry sauce and applesauce. Pour into a 6-cup ring mold coated with cooking spray. Cover and refrigerate overnight. Unmold onto a serving platter.

Nutrition Information

- Calories: 134 calories
- Total Fat: 0 g
- Cholesterol: 0 mg
- Sodium: 41mg
- Total Carbohydrate: 34g
- Protein: 1g
- Fiber: 1g

10. ApplesauceRaspberry Gelatin Mold

"The children in our families especially enjoy this tangy, refreshing salad, and its pretty, bright red color makes it a festive addition to a special occasion meal". – Kathy Spang, Manheim, Pennsylvania

Serving: 10 servings. | Prep: 10 m | Cook: 5 m | Ready in: 15 m

Ingredients

- 3 cups unsweetened applesauce
- 1/4 cup orange juice
- 2 packages (3 ounces each) raspberry gelatin
- 1-1/2 cups lemon-lime soda

Direction

- In a large saucepan, bring applesauce and orange juice to a boil. Remove from the heat; stir in gelatin until dissolved. Slowly add soda.
- Pour into a 6-cup mold coated with cooking spray. Refrigerate until firm. Unmold onto a serving platter.

Nutrition Information

- Calories: 111 calories
- Total Fat: 0 g
- Cholesterol: 0 mg
- Sodium: 44mg
- Total Carbohydrate: 27g
- Protein: 2g
- Fiber: 1g

11. Apricot Aspic

A family who usually passes up molded salads will hunt for this fruity version at our covered dish buffet. Not only is it delicious, it adds color to any meal.

Serving: 10 servings. | Prep: 15 m | Cook: 0 m | Ready in: 15 m

Ingredients

- 2 cans (16 ounces each) apricot halves
- Pinch salt
- 2 packages (3 ounces each) orange gelatin
- 1 can (6 ounces) frozen orange juice concentrate, thawed
- 1 tablespoon lemon juice
- 1 cup lemon-lime soda

Direction

- Drain apricots, reserving 1-1/2 cups juice; set apricots aside. In a small saucepan over medium heat, bring apricot juice and salt to a boil. Remove from the heat; add gelatin and stir until dissolved.

- In a blender, process apricots, orange juice concentrate and lemon juice until smooth. Add to gelatin mixture along with soda; mix well. Pour into a 6-cup mold that has been sprayed with cooking spray. Chill until firm.

Nutrition Information

- Calories: 93 calories
- Total Fat: 0 g
- Cholesterol: 0 mg
- Sodium: 55mg
- Total Carbohydrate: 21g
- Protein: 1g
- Fiber: 0 g

12. Apricot Gelatin Mold

My mother always made this apricot Jell-O salad for celebrations. When my husband and I were dating, he fell in love with this dish and, as soon as we were married, asked me to get the recipe. You can substitute peach or orange gelatin for a fresh summer treat. --Suzanne Holcomb, St. Johnsville, New York

Serving: 12 servings (1/2 cup each). | Prep: 20 m | Cook: 5 m | Ready in: 25 m

Ingredients

- 1 can (8 ounces) unsweetened crushed pineapple
- 2 packages (3 ounces each) apricot or peach gelatin
- 1 package (8 ounces) reduced-fat cream cheese
- 3/4 cup grated carrots
- 1 carton (8 ounces) frozen fat-free whipped topping, thawed

Direction

- Drain pineapple, reserving juice in a 2-cup measuring cup; add enough water to measure 2 cups. Set pineapple aside. Pour juice mixture into a small saucepan. Bring to a boil; remove

from heat. Dissolve gelatin in juice mixture. Cool for 10 minutes.

- In a large bowl, beat cream cheese until creamy. Gradually add gelatin mixture, beating until smooth. Refrigerate for 30-40 minutes or until slightly thickened.
- Fold in pineapple and carrots, then whipped topping. Transfer to an 8-cup ring mold coated with cooking spray. Refrigerate until set. Unmold onto a serving platter.

Nutrition Information

- Calories: 144 calories
- Total Fat: 4g
- Cholesterol: 13mg
- Sodium: 128mg
- Total Carbohydrate: 23g
- Protein: 3g
- Fiber: 0 g

13. Apricot Gelatin Salad

I serve this smooth, fluffy salad all year for special meals, but it's so pleasant around Eastertime with its pretty color and fruity flavor. The apricot pieces are an unexpected treat. -- Ellen Benninger, Stoneboro, Pennsylvania

Serving: 12-16 servings. | Prep: 20 m | Cook: 0 m | Ready in: 20 m

Ingredients

- 1 package (6 ounces) apricot or orange gelatin
- 2 cups boiling water
- 1 can (20 ounces) crushed pineapple
- 1 package (8 ounces) cream cheese, softened
- 1 can (15 ounces) apricot halves, drained and chopped
- 1/2 cup chopped walnuts
- 1 carton (8 ounces) frozen whipped topping, thawed
- Additional chopped walnuts, optional

Direction

- In a bowl, dissolve gelatin in water. Drain pineapple, reserving juice. Add pineapple to gelatin and set aside. In a bowl, beat cream cheese and pineapple juice until smooth. Stir in gelatin mixture; chill until partially set, stirring occasionally. Stir in apricots and walnuts. Fold in whipped topping. Pour into a 13x9-in. dish. Sprinkle with walnuts if desired. Chill until firm.

Nutrition Information

- Calories: 167 calories
- Total Fat: 10g
- Cholesterol: 16mg
- Sodium: 44mg
- Total Carbohydrate: 18g
- Protein: 2g
- Fiber: 1g

14. Apricot Orange Gelatin Salad

This delicious salad adds color to any table with its combination of fruity-fizzy ingredients.

Serving: 10 servings. | Prep: 15 m | Cook: 0 m | Ready in: 15 m

Ingredients

- 2 cans (16 ounces each) apricot halves
- Dash salt
- 2 packages (3 ounces each) orange gelatin
- 1 can (6 ounces) frozen orange juice concentrate, thawed
- 1 tablespoon lemon juice
- 1 cup lemon-lime soda

Direction

- Drain apricots, reserving 1-1/2 cups juice; set apricots aside. In a small saucepan, bring apricot juice and salt to a boil over medium heat. Remove from the heat; add gelatin, stirring until gelatin is dissolved.

- In a blender, combine the orange juice concentrate, lemon juice and reserved apricots; cover and process until smooth. Add to gelatin mixture along with soda; mix well. Pour into a 6-cup mold coated with cooking spray. Cover and refrigerate until firm. Unmold and transfer to a serving plate.

Nutrition Information

- Calories: 181 calories
- Total Fat: 0 g
- Cholesterol: 0 mg
- Sodium: 60mg
- Total Carbohydrate: 45g
- Protein: 3g
- Fiber: 2g

15. Asian Veggie Gelatin

While trying the offerings at a salad potluck, I was excited to sample this refreshing dish. It's a nice change from sweeter gelatin salads. The "secret ingredient" is soy sauce.

Serving: 4 servings. | Prep: 15 m | Cook: 0 m | Ready in: 15 m

Ingredients

- 1 package (.3 ounce) sugar-free orange gelatin
- 3/4 cup boiling water
- 1 cup cold water
- 4-1/2 teaspoons reduced-sodium soy sauce
- 1 tablespoon lemon juice
- 1/2 cup canned bean sprouts
- 1/2 cup sliced celery
- 1/2 cup shredded carrots
- 1/4 cup sliced water chestnuts, halved
- 1 tablespoon chopped green onion

Direction

- In a large bowl, dissolve gelatin in boiling water. Stir in the cold water, soy sauce and lemon juice. Add the bean sprouts, celery, carrots, water chestnuts and onion; mix well.

- Spoon into four 6-oz. bowls coated with cooking spray. Refrigerate for 1 hour or until set. Invert onto salad plates.

Nutrition Information

- Calories: 30 calories
- Total Fat: 0 g
- Cholesterol: 0 mg
- Sodium: 307mg
- Total Carbohydrate: 5g
- Protein: 2g
- Fiber: 1g

16. Beet Salad

We live in the high-mountain country of central Idaho, where the cool climate is idea for root crops like beets. This beet recipe came from a friend many years ago, and it remains one of my favorite party dishes. It's a particularly colorful and refreshing salad to serve at a ladies luncheon or as a tasty complement to a meat dish.

Serving: 9-12 servings. | Prep: 15 m | Cook: 0 m | Ready in: 15 m

Ingredients

- 1 can (16 ounces) diced or julienned beets
- 2 packages (3 ounces each) lemon gelatin
- 1-1/2 cups cold water
- 2 tablespoons finely chopped onion
- 1 to 2 tablespoons prepared horseradish
- 4 teaspoons white vinegar
- 1/4 teaspoon salt
- 1-1/2 cups chopped celery
- 1/4 cup sliced pimiento-stuffed olives
- Lettuce leaves, mayonnaise and sliced pimiento-stuffed olives, optional

Direction

- Drain beets, reserving liquid in a 2-cup measuring cup; add enough water to measure 2 cups. Set beets aside. Place beet juice mixture in a large saucepan; bring to a boil. Remove from the heat; stir in gelatin until dissolved.

Add the cold water, onion, horseradish, vinegar and salt. Chill until partially set.
- Stir in the celery, olives and reserved beets. Pour into an 8-in. square dish. Chill until firm, about 3 hours. Cut salad into squares. If desired, serve on a lettuce-lined plate and top with a dollop of mayonnaise and an olive.

Nutrition Information

- Calories: 47 calories
- Total Fat: 1g
- Cholesterol: 0 mg
- Sodium: 216mg
- Total Carbohydrate: 10g
- Protein: 1g
- Fiber: 1g

17. Berry Gelatin Mold

This refreshing gelatin mold is delicious and always a big hit! For a patriotic buffet, I add a scoop of frozen whipped topping, then place a fancy-cut strawberry and a sprinkling of blueberries for festive, red-white-and-blue color. --Anne Marie Papineau, Hanover, Connecticut

Serving: 8 servings. | Prep: 15 m | Cook: 0 m | Ready in: 15 m

Ingredients

- 2 packages (3 ounces each) strawberry gelatin
- 2 cups boiling cranberry juice
- 1-1/2 cups club soda, chilled
- 1 teaspoon lemon juice
- 1 cup each fresh blueberries, raspberries and sliced strawberries
- Lettuce leaves
- Additional mixed fresh berries, optional

Direction

- In a large bowl, dissolve gelatin in boiling cranberry juice. Let stand for 10 minutes. Stir in club soda and lemon juice; refrigerate for 45 minutes or until partially set.

- Fold in berries. Pour into a 6-cup ring mold coated with cooking spray. Refrigerate for 4 hours or until set. Unmold onto a lettuce-lined platter; fill center with additional berries if desired.

Nutrition Information

- Calories: 131 calories
- Total Fat: 0 g
- Cholesterol: 0 mg
- Sodium: 59mg
- Total Carbohydrate: 32g
- Protein: 3g
- Fiber: 2g

18. Berry Gelatin Ring

Cranberries give extra holiday appeal to this gelatin salad sent in by Elise Spring of Bellevue, Ohio. "A co-worker always shares this festive fruit ring with us at staff potlucks," she relates.

Serving: 8 servings. | Prep: 15 m | Cook: 0 m | Ready in: 15 m

Ingredients

- 1 package (6 ounces) raspberry gelatin
- 2 cups boiling water
- 1 can (14 ounces) whole-berry cranberry sauce
- 1 can (8 ounces) crushed pineapple, undrained
- 1/2 cup red wine or grape juice
- 1/3 cup chopped walnuts
- 1 package (8 ounces) cream cheese, softened
- 1/4 cup mayonnaise
- 1 teaspoon grated orange zest

Direction

- In a large bowl, dissolve gelatin in water. Add the cranberry sauce, pineapple, wine and walnuts. Chill until partially set, about 2 hours.
- Pour into a 6-cup ring mold coated with cooking spray. Refrigerate until set. Unmold onto a serving plate. In a small bowl, combine

the cream cheese, mayonnaise and orange zest. Serve with the salad.

Nutrition Information

- Calories: 367 calories
- Total Fat: 18g
- Cholesterol: 34mg
- Sodium: 183mg
- Total Carbohydrate: 46g
- Protein: 5g
- Fiber: 1g

19. Best Rosy Rhubarb Mold

Any meal benefits from this ruby-colored salad - it's always a refreshing accompaniment. I never have leftovers, since the combination of sweet, tangy and crunchy ingredients is so irresistible. -Regina Albright, Southhaven, Mississippi

Serving: 12 servings. | Prep: 25 m | Cook: 0 m | Ready in: 25 m

Ingredients

- 4 cups chopped fresh or frozen rhubarb
- 1 cup water
- 2/3 cup sugar
- 1/4 teaspoon salt
- 1 package (6 ounces) strawberry gelatin
- 1-1/2 cups cold water
- 1/4 cup lemon juice
- 2 cans (11 ounces each) mandarin oranges, drained
- 1 cup chopped celery
- Optional garnishes: lettuce leaves, sliced strawberries, green grapes, sour cream and ground nutmeg

Direction

- In a saucepan, combine rhubarb, water, sugar and salt; bring to a boil over medium heat. Boil for 1-2 minutes or until the rhubarb is tender; remove from the heat. Stir in gelatin until dissolved. Stir in cold water and lemon juice. Chill until partially set. Fold in oranges and celery. Pour into a 6-cup mold or an 8-in. square dish that has been coated with cooking spray. Chill until set. Unmold onto lettuce leaves or cut into squares. If desired, garnish with fruit and serve with sour cream sprinkled with nutmeg.

Nutrition Information

- Calories: 79 calories
- Total Fat: 0 g
- Cholesterol: 0 mg
- Sodium: 98mg
- Total Carbohydrate: 19g
- Protein: 2g
- Fiber: 0 g

20. Best Rosy Rhubarb Salad

During the holidays, I'll at times serve this unusual salad in place of cranberry sauce. It goes well with pork or poultry . Honestly, though, it's good with any everyday meal, too. It's just a little tart, so it rounds out rich food. I've been cooking ever since I made corn bread to surprise my family when I was 9. My brothers wouldn't eat it--but my parents did! My husband and I are dairy farmers in partnership with our grown son.

Serving: 8 servings. | Prep: 20 m | Cook: 0 m | Ready in: 20 m

Ingredients

- 3 cups sliced fresh or frozen rhubarb (1-inch pieces)
- 1 tablespoon sugar
- 1 package (3 ounces) raspberry gelatin
- 1 cup unsweetened pineapple juice
- 1 teaspoon lemon juice
- 1 cup diced peeled apples
- 1 cup diced celery
- 1/4 cup chopped pecans

Direction

- In a medium saucepan, cook and stir rhubarb and sugar over medium-low heat until rhubarb is soft and tender. Remove from the heat; add gelatin and stir until dissolved. Stir

in pineapple and lemon juices. Chill until partially set.
- Stir in apples, celery and pecans. Pour into a 4-1/2 cup mold coated with cooking spray or glass bowl. Chill several hours or overnight.

Nutrition Information

- Calories: 108 calories
- Total Fat: 3g
- Cholesterol: 0 mg
- Sodium: 39mg
- Total Carbohydrate: 20g
- Protein: 2g
- Fiber: 2g

21. Blueberry Raspberry Gelatin

In Fortuna, California, Judy Scott whips up this pretty dessert that features plenty of fresh blueberries.

Serving: 6 servings. | Prep: 20 m | Cook: 0 m | Ready in: 20 m

Ingredients

- 1 package (.3 ounce) sugar-free raspberry gelatin
- 1 cup boiling water
- 3/4 cup cold water
- 1 cup fresh or frozen unsweetened blueberries, thawed
- TOPPING:
- 2 ounces reduced-fat cream cheese
- 1/4 cup fat-free sour cream
- Sugar substitute equivalent to 2 teaspoons sugar
- 1/2 teaspoon vanilla extract
- 2 tablespoons chopped pecans, toasted

Direction

- In a small bowl, dissolve gelatin in boiling water. Stir in cold water. Cover and refrigerate until partially set. Fold in blueberries. Transfer to an 8x4-in. loaf pan coated with cooking spray. Cover and refrigerate for 1 hour or until set.

- For topping, in a small bowl, beat the cream cheese and sour cream until smooth. Stir in the sugar substitute and vanilla. Unmold gelatin; cut into six slices. Top each slice with topping and pecans.

Nutrition Information

- Calories: 72 calories
- Total Fat: 4g
- Cholesterol: 8mg
- Sodium: 80mg
- Total Carbohydrate: 6g
- Protein: 3g
- Fiber: 1g

22. Broken Glass Gelatin

A lightened-up version of an old classic, this fancy, colorful recipe from Dorothy Alexander in Martin, Tennessee is pretty enough to double as a light dessert!

Serving: 15 servings. | Prep: 30 m | Cook: 10 m | Ready in: 40 m

Ingredients

- 1-1/2 cups reduced-fat graham cracker crumbs (about 8 whole crackers)
- 7 tablespoons sugar, divided
- 5 tablespoons reduced-fat butter, melted
- 1 cup unsweetened pineapple juice
- 1 envelope unflavored gelatin
- 1 package (.3 ounce) sugar-free orange gelatin
- 4-1/2 cups boiling water, divided
- 1 package (.3 ounce) sugar-free lime gelatin
- 1 package (.3 ounce) sugar-free strawberry gelatin
- 1 carton (8 ounces) frozen reduced-fat whipped topping, thawed

Direction

- In a large bowl, combine the cracker crumbs, 5 tablespoons sugar and butter; press into an ungreased 13x9-in. dish. Chill.

- In a small saucepan, combine pineapple juice and remaining sugar. Sprinkle unflavored gelatin over juice mixture; let stand for 1 minute. Heat over low heat, stirring until gelatin is completely dissolved. Transfer to a large bowl; cool.
- Dissolve orange gelatin in 1-1/2 cups boiling water; pour into an 8x4-in. loaf pan coated with cooking spray. Refrigerate until firm. Repeat with lime and strawberry gelatins and remaining boiling water, using additional loaf pans.
- Gently fold whipped topping into pineapple juice mixture; cover and refrigerate. Cut flavored gelatins into 1-in. cubes; gently fold into whipped topping mixture. Spoon over crust. Refrigerate for several hours or overnight.

Nutrition Information

- Calories: 98 calories
- Total Fat: 4g
- Cholesterol: 7mg
- Sodium: 78mg
- Total Carbohydrate: 13g
- Protein: 2g
- Fiber: 0 g

23. CabbageCucumber Gelatin Cups

When we have fresh cabbage and cucumbers from the garden, this is one of my favorite salads to make for Sunday dinner. But with fresh produce available year-round, it's good anytime.

Serving: 4 servings. | Prep: 10 m | Cook: 0 m | Ready in: 10 m

Ingredients

- 1 package (3 ounces) lime gelatin
- 1 cup boiling water
- 1/2 cup mayonnaise
- 1 cup shredded cabbage
- 1/2 cup chopped cucumber
- 2 tablespoons chopped green pepper

Direction

- In a bowl, dissolve gelatin in boiling water. Whisk in the mayonnaise until smooth. Stir in the cabbage, cucumber and green pepper. Pour into four custard cups. Cover and refrigerate until firm.

Nutrition Information

- Calories: 284 calories
- Total Fat: 22g
- Cholesterol: 10mg
- Sodium: 202mg
- Total Carbohydrate: 20g
- Protein: 2g
- Fiber: 1g

24. Cherry Coke Salad

This sparkling salad was as popular at my sister's party as the cherry-flavored cola was back in the 1950s.--Judy Nix, Toccoa, Georgia

Serving: 10-12 servings. | Prep: 10 m | Cook: 0 m | Ready in: 10 m

Ingredients

- 1 can (20 ounces) crushed pineapple
- 1/2 cup water
- 2 packages (3 ounces each) cherry gelatin
- 1 can (21 ounces) cherry pie filling
- 3/4 cup cola

Direction

- Drain pineapple, reserving juice; set fruit aside. In a saucepan or microwave, bring pineapple juice and water to a boil. Add gelatin; stir until dissolved. Stir in pie filling and cola.
- Pour into a serving bowl. Refrigerate until slightly thickened. Fold in reserved pineapple. Refrigerate until firm.

Nutrition Information

- Calories: 118 calories
- Total Fat: 0 g
- Cholesterol: 0 mg
- Sodium: 26mg
- Total Carbohydrate: 29g
- Protein: 1g
- Fiber: 1g

25. Cherry Cola Salad

This tempting gelatin salad has a big cherry flavor and a fun zing from the cola. My two small children are always happy to see this salad on the table. We think it tastes great with or without the whipped topping.

Serving: 8-10 servings. | Prep: 10 m | Cook: 0 m | Ready in: 10 m

Ingredients

- 1 package (6 ounces) cherry gelatin
- 1-1/2 cups boiling water
- 1-1/2 cups carbonated cola beverage
- 1 can (21 ounces) cherry pie filling
- Whipped topping, optional

Direction

- Dissolve gelatin in water. Add cola and pie filling; mix well. Pour into an 8-in. square baking dish. Refrigerate until firm. Garnish with whipped topping if desired.

Nutrition Information

- Calories: 146 calories
- Total Fat: 0 g
- Cholesterol: 0 mg
- Sodium: 51mg
- Total Carbohydrate: 35g
- Protein: 2g
- Fiber: 0 g

26. Cherry Cranberry Salad

Not a Christmas goes by that Deb Amrine doesn't fix this bright molded salad. "I've taken it to many holiday dinners, and everyone loves it--even people who don't usually enjoy cranberries," she reports from Grand Haven, Michigan.

Serving: 12-16 servings. | Prep: 15 m | Cook: 0 m | Ready in: 15 m

Ingredients

- 1 package (6 ounces) cherry gelatin
- 1 cup sugar
- 2 cups boiling water
- 1 can (20 ounces) crushed pineapple, undrained
- 3 cups fresh or frozen cranberries, chopped
- 1-1/2 cups diced apples
- 1 cup chopped celery
- 1 cup chopped walnuts

Direction

- In a large bowl, combine gelatin and sugar. Add water; stir until gelatin and sugar are dissolved. Stir in pineapple, cranberries, apples, celery and walnuts. Pour into a 2-qt. serving bowl; cover and refrigerate for 3-4 hours until set.

Nutrition Information

- Calories: 173 calories
- Total Fat: 5g
- Cholesterol: 0 mg
- Sodium: 31mg
- Total Carbohydrate: 33g
- Protein: 3g
- Fiber: 2g

27. Cherry Gelatin Fruit Salad

In her Memphis, Tennessee home, Margaret McNeil jazzes up cherry gelatin with three pantry staples to create this sweet sensation. The no-fuss salad can be assembled in just 10 minutes. Then, let it firm up in the refrigerator.

Serving: 8 servings. | Prep: 10 m | Cook: 0 m | Ready in: 10 m

Ingredients

- 1 cup applesauce
- 2 packages (3 ounces each) cherry gelatin
- 1 can (12 ounces) lemon-lime soda
- 1 can (8 ounces) crushed pineapple, undrained

Direction

- In a large saucepan, bring applesauce to a boil. Remove from the heat; stir in gelatin until dissolved. Slowly add soda and pineapple. Pour into a 1-1/2 qt. serving bowl. Refrigerate until firm.

Nutrition Information

- Calories: 102 calories
- Total Fat: 0 g
- Cholesterol: 0 mg
- Sodium: 30mg
- Total Carbohydrate: 26g
- Protein: 1g
- Fiber: 1g

28. Cherry Gelatin Salad with Bananas

This pretty, molded salad was always on my birthday menu. I love the chunks of banana, the cherry flavor and the festive red color. It's ideal for holiday menus. — Joann Jensen (daughter), Lowell, Indiana

Serving: 6 servings. | Prep: 15 m | Cook: 0 m | Ready in: 15 m

Ingredients

- 1 can (15 ounces) pitted dark sweet cherries
- 1 package (3 ounces) cherry gelatin
- 1 cup cold water

- 1 tablespoon lemon juice
- 2 medium bananas, sliced
- 1/4 cup chopped pecans
- Additonal sliced banana and chopped pecans, optional

Direction

- Drain cherries, reserving liquid in a 1-cup measuring cup; add enough water to measure 1 cup. In a small saucepan, bring mixture to a boil. Remove from the heat; stir in gelatin until dissolved. Stir in cold water and lemon juice.
- Cover and refrigerate until syrupy, about 40 minutes. Fold in the bananas, pecans and cherries. Transfer to a 6-cup mold coated with cooking spray. Refrigerate until firm.
- Unmold onto a serving platter. Garnish with additional banana and pecans if desired.

Nutrition Information

- Calories: 169 calories
- Total Fat: 4g
- Cholesterol: 0 mg
- Sodium: 35mg
- Total Carbohydrate: 34g
- Protein: 3g
- Fiber: 3g

29. Cherry Gelatin Squares

"I like to take advantage of gelatin mixes and pie fillings to make colorful salads that can be prepared the day before you need them," remarks Chris Rentmeister from Ripon, Wisconsin. "These fruity squares are great for everyday suppers yet special enough for company."

Serving: 9 servings. | Prep: 15 m | Cook: 0 m | Ready in: 15 m

Ingredients

- 2 packages (3 ounces each) cherry gelatin
- 1-1/2 cups boiling water
- 1 can (21 ounces) cherry pie filling
- 1-1/4 cups lemon-lime soda, chilled

- Whipped topping, optional

Direction

- In a large bowl, dissolve gelatin in water. Stir in pie filling and mix well. Slowly stir in soda (mixture will foam).
- Pour into an 8-in. square dish. Cover and refrigerate until firm. Cut into squares. Garnish with whipped topping if desired.

Nutrition Information

- Calories: 68 calories
- Total Fat: 1g
- Cholesterol: 0 mg
- Sodium: 115mg
- Total Carbohydrate: 13g
- Protein: 2g
- Fiber: 0 g

30. Cherry Pineapple Salad

This recipe makes a really pretty salad. My sister-in-law often brings it to our family get-togethers on holidays and special occasions. --Leona Luecking, West Burlington, Iowa

Serving: 12-16 servings. | Prep: 20 m | Cook: 0 m | Ready in: 20 m

Ingredients

- 3 packages (3 ounces each) cherry gelatin
- 2-1/3 cups boiling water
- 2 cans (16-1/2 ounces each) pitted dark sweet cherries
- 1 can (20 ounces) pineapple tidbits
- 1/3 cup lemon juice
- 1/3 cup heavy whipping cream
- 1/3 cup mayonnaise
- 6 ounces cream cheese, softened
- Dash salt
- 1/2 cup coarsely chopped nuts

Direction

- In a large bowl, dissolve gelatin in water. Drain fruits, reserving enough cherry and pineapple juices to measure 2-1/2 cups; add to gelatin with lemon juice. Set fruits aside.
- Divide gelatin mixture in half. Set aside one portion of gelatin at room temperature; chill the other portion until partially set. Fold pineapple into chilled gelatin; pour into a 13x9-in. dish. Chill until almost firm.
- In a small bowl, beat the cream, mayonnaise, cream cheese and salt until light and fluffy. Spread over chilled gelatin layer. Refrigerate until firm. Chill reserved gelatin mixture until partially set. Fold in cherries and nuts; spread over cream cheese layer. Chill for at least 3 hours.

Nutrition Information

- Calories: 151 calories
- Total Fat: 10g
- Cholesterol: 14mg
- Sodium: 65mg
- Total Carbohydrate: 16g
- Protein: 2g
- Fiber: 1g

31. Cherry Ribbon Salad

Filled with pineapple, pecans and cherry pie filling, this colorful salad mold adds fun, fruity flavor to any potluck menu. – Virginia Luke, Red Level, Alabama

Serving: 12 servings. | Prep: 10 m | Cook: 0 m | Ready in: 10 m

Ingredients

- 1 package (3 ounces) cherry gelatin
- 2-1/4 cups boiling water, divided
- 1 can (21 ounces) cherry pie filling
- 1 package (3 ounces) orange gelatin
- 1 can (8 ounces) crushed pineapple, undrained
- 1 cup whipped topping
- 1/3 cup mayonnaise

- 1/4 cup chopped pecans, optional

Direction

- In a large bowl, dissolve cherry gelatin in 1-1/4 cups boiling water. Stir in pie filling. Pour into a 7-cup ring mold coated with cooking spray; refrigerate for about 1 hour or until thickened but not set.
- In a large bowl, dissolve orange gelatin in remaining boiling water. Stir in pineapple. Chill for about 1 hour or until thickened but not set.
- Combine the whipped topping, mayonnaise and pecans if desired; fold into orange mixture. Spoon over cherry layer. Refrigerate for at least 1 hour or until firm. Unmold onto a serving plate.

Nutrition Information

- Calories: 184 calories
- Total Fat: 6g
- Cholesterol: 2mg
- Sodium: 75mg
- Total Carbohydrate: 31g
- Protein: 2g
- Fiber: 0 g

32. CherryCheese Gelatin Salad

THIS recipe was in a community cookbook compiled by our high school's booster club 22 years ago. The measurements and directions were vague so I experimented until I got it right. This is a pretty salad to serve at luncheons and the flavor is light. --Karen Ann Bland, Gove, Kansas

Serving: 5 servings. | Prep: 15 m | Cook: 5 m | Ready in: 20 m

Ingredients

- 1 can (20 ounces) unsweetened pineapple chunks
- 1 can (15 ounces) pitted dark sweet cherries
- 1 package (3 ounces) cherry gelatin
- 3 ounces cream cheese, softened

- 1/2 teaspoon sugar
- 2 tablespoons chopped pecans
- 1 drop almond extract
- 5 lettuce leaves

Direction

- Drain pineapple and cherries, reserving juices in a 2-cup measuring cup; add enough water to measure 2 cups. Set fruit aside.
- In a small saucepan, bring juice mixture to a boil over medium heat. Remove from the heat; stir in gelatin until dissolved. Cover and refrigerate until partially set.
- In a small bowl, combine the cream cheese, sugar, pecans and extract. Shape into 3/4-in. balls. Gently fold cheese balls and cherries into gelatin mixture. Transfer to five 1-cup molds coated with cooking spray. Refrigerate until firm.
- Unmold onto lettuce-lined plates; arrange pineapple chunks around gelatin.

Nutrition Information

- Calories: 258 calories
- Total Fat: 8g
- Cholesterol: 19mg
- Sodium: 102mg
- Total Carbohydrate: 45g
- Protein: 4g
- Fiber: 3g

33. Christmas Cranberry Salad

You might find that this yummy gelatin salad is one side dish pretty enough to steal top billing! It's cool, crunchy and refreshing and adds a splash of Christmas color to any table. Garnish with lettuce, orange slices and sugared cranberries.

Serving: 12 servings. | Prep: 20 m | Cook: 0 m | Ready in: 20 m

Ingredients

- 1-1/2 cups chopped fresh or frozen cranberries
- 1/2 cup sugar
- 2 packages (3 ounces each) orange or lemon gelatin
- 1/4 teaspoon salt
- 2 cups boiling water
- 1-1/2 cups cold water
- 1 tablespoon lemon juice
- 1/4 teaspoon ground cinnamon
- 1/8 teaspoon ground cloves
- 1 medium navel orange, peeled and diced
- 1/2 cup chopped almonds
- Lettuce leaves

Direction

- In a small bowl, combine cranberries and sugar; set aside. In a large bowl, dissolve gelatin and salt in boiling water. Stir in the cold water, lemon juice, cinnamon and cloves. Cover and chill for 1 hour.
- Stir in the orange, almonds and cranberry mixture. Pour into a 6-cup ring mold coated with cooking spray. Cover and refrigerate for 3-4 hours or until set. Invert onto a lettuce-lined serving plate.

Nutrition Information

- Calories:
- Total Fat: g
- Cholesterol: mg
- Sodium: mg
- Total Carbohydrate: g
- Protein: g
- Fiber: g

34. Christmas Gelatin Ring

This colorful salad with its red and green layers is fun to serve for a festive dinner or brunch. It's been my family's favorite for many years- everyone loves the Jell-O and cream cheese combination. It goes with all kinds of entrees.

Serving: 12 servings. | Prep: 30 m | Cook: 0 m | Ready in: 30 m

Ingredients

- 1 package (3 ounces) cherry gelatin
- 3 cups boiling water, divided
- 1 can (29 ounces) sliced pears, undrained
- 1 package (3 ounces) lemon gelatin
- 1 package (8 ounces) cream cheese, cubed and softened
- 1 package (3 ounces) lime gelatin
- 1 can (20 ounces) crushed pineapple

Direction

- In a bowl, dissolve cherry gelatin in 1 cup boiling water. Drain pears, reserving 1 cup juice (discard remaining juice or save for another use). Stir pears and reserved juice into cherry gelatin. Pour into a 10-in. fluted tube pan or 3-qt. ring mold coated with cooking spray. Refrigerate until nearly set, about 1-1/4 hours.
- In a bowl, dissolve the lemon gelatin in 1 cup boiling water; refrigerate until slightly thickened. Beat in the cream cheese until blended. Pour over the cherry layer.
- In another bowl, dissolve lime gelatin in remaining boiling water. Drain pineapple well, reserving juice. Add enough water to juice to measure 3/4 cup. Stir pineapple and reserved juice into lime gelatin; spoon over lemon layer. Refrigerate until firm. Unmold onto a serving plate.

Nutrition Information

- Calories: 215 calories
- Total Fat: 7g
- Cholesterol: 21mg
- Sodium: 110mg
- Total Carbohydrate: 37g
- Protein: 4g
- Fiber: 1g

35. Christmas Ribbon Salad

Spirits are light at holiday time around Debra Stoner's home--and so are many of the meas she serves. "I make this dessert every year at Christmas," she informs from Carlisle, Pennsylvania. "It's one of my husband's favorites. I slimmed down the recipe by using sugar-free gelatin and reduced-fat topping."

Serving: 15 servings. | Prep: 20 m | Cook: 0 m | Ready in: 20 m

Ingredients

- 2 packages (.3 ounce each) sugar-free lime gelatin
- 5 cups boiling water, divided
- 4 cups cold water, divided
- 2 packages (.3 ounce each) sugar-free lemon gelatin
- 1 package (8 ounces) reduced-fat cream cheese, cubed
- 1 can (8 ounces) crushed pineapple, undrained
- 1/4 cup chopped pecans
- 2 cups reduced-fat whipped topping
- 2 packages (.3 ounce each) sugar-free cherry gelatin

Direction

- In a bowl, dissolve lime gelatin in 2 cups boiling water. Add 2 cups cold water; stir. Pour into a 13-in. x 9-in. dish coated with cooking spray. Refrigerate until almost set, about 2 hours.
- In a bowl, dissolve lemon gelatin in 1 cup boiling water; whisk in cream cheese until smooth. Stir in pineapple and pecans. Fold in whipped topping. Spoon over first layer. Refrigerate until firm, about 1 hour.

- In a bowl, dissolve cherry gelatin in remaining boiling water. Add remaining cold water; stir. Chill until syrupy and slightly thickened. Carefully spoon over second layer. Refrigerate until set, about 4 hours.

Nutrition Information

- Calories: 92 calories
- Total Fat: 5g
- Cholesterol: 8mg
- Sodium: 140mg
- Total Carbohydrate: 5g
- Protein: 3g
- Fiber: 1g

36. Christmas Wreath Salad

It's a jolly holiday when Mom makes this cool eye-catching salad. Pecans, pineapple and maraschino cherries are sweet surprises in every serving of this pretty side dish. -Becky Brunette, Minneapolis, Minnesota

Serving: 6 servings. | Prep: 10 m | Cook: 0 m | Ready in: 10 m

Ingredients

- 1 package (6 ounces) strawberry gelatin
- 1 cup boiling water
- 1 can (20 ounces) crushed pineapple
- 1 cup (8 ounces) plain yogurt
- 1 cup chopped pecans, optional
- 1/2 cup red maraschino cherries, halved
- Lettuce leaves and additional cherries, optional

Direction

- In a large bowl, dissolve gelatin in boiling water. Refrigerate until partially set, about 30 minutes. Drain pineapple, reserving juice; set pineapple aside. Add enough cold water to juice to measure 1-3/4 cups; stir into gelatin mixture. Whisk in yogurt until smooth. Fold in nuts if desired, cherries and reserved pineapple.

- Pour into a 2-qt. ring mold coated with cooking spray. Refrigerate until set. Unmold onto a lettuce-lined serving plate and garnish with additional cherries if desired.

Nutrition Information

- Calories: 212 calories
- Total Fat: 1g
- Cholesterol: 5mg
- Sodium: 93mg
- Total Carbohydrate: 48g
- Protein: 4g
- Fiber: 1g

37. Chunky Cranberry Salad

I found this recipe while taking a cooking class. Full of mixed fruit, celery and nuts, it's a lively alternative to jellied cranberry sauce. When cranberries are in season, I buy extra and freeze them so I can make this salad year-round.

Serving: 12 servings. | Prep: 10 m | Cook: 15 m | Ready in: 25 m

Ingredients

- 4 cups fresh or frozen cranberries
- 3-1/2 cups unsweetened pineapple juice
- 2 envelopes unflavored gelatin
- 1/2 cup cold water
- 2 cups sugar
- 1 can (20 ounces) unsweetened pineapple tidbits, drained
- 1 cup chopped pecans
- 1 cup green grapes, chopped
- 1/2 cup finely chopped celery
- 2 teaspoons grated orange zest

Direction

- In a large saucepan, combine the cranberries and pineapple juice. Cook over medium heat until berries pop, about 15 minutes.
- Meanwhile, in a small bowl, sprinkle gelatin over cold water; let stand for 5 minutes. In a

large bowl, combine the berry mixture, sugar and softened gelatin. Chill until partially set.
- Fold in the pineapple, pecans, grapes, celery and orange zest. Pour into individual serving dishes. Chill until firm.

Nutrition Information

- Calories: 288 calories
- Total Fat: 7g
- Cholesterol: 0 mg
- Sodium: 9mg
- Total Carbohydrate: 57g
- Protein: 3g
- Fiber: 3g

38. Cider Cranberry Salad

"The area we live in grows lots of cranberries, and we really like them," comments Barbara Taylor of Ocean Park, Washington. Her tasty gelatin salad has lovely orange and apple flavors that accent the tart cranberry sauce.

Serving: 6-8 servings. | Prep: 5 m | Cook: 0 m | Ready in: 5 m

Ingredients

- 1 package (3 ounces) orange gelatin
- 3/4 cup boiling apple cider
- 3/4 cup cold apple cider
- 1 can (14 ounces) whole-berry cranberry sauce

Direction

- In a bowl, dissolve gelatin in boiling cider. Stir in cold cider and cranberry sauce. Pour into individual dishes. Chill until firm.

Nutrition Information

- Calories: 142 calories
- Total Fat: 0 g
- Cholesterol: 0 mg
- Sodium: 41mg
- Total Carbohydrate: 36g
- Protein: 1g

- Fiber: 1g

39. Cinnamon Apple Salad

THIS RECIPE came from my mother. It's a family favorite and one I took with me when I left home. The color complements the holiday season. It's very pretty when cut into squares and served on a lettuce-lined plate. I also like that I can fix it a day ahead of time, especially when preparing a big holiday meal. -Lisa Andis, Morristown, Indiana

Serving: 9 servings. | Prep: 15 m | Cook: 0 m | Ready in: 15 m

Ingredients

- 1/2 cup red-hot candies
- 1 cup boiling water
- 1 package (3 ounces) lemon gelatin
- 1 cup applesauce
- 1 package (8 ounces) cream cheese, softened
- 1/2 cup Miracle Whip
- 1/2 cup chopped pecans
- 1/4 cup chopped celery

Direction

- In a bowl, dissolve candies in water (reheat if necessary). Add gelatin; stir to dissolve. Stir in applesauce. Pour half into an 8-in. square pan that has been lightly coated with cooking spray. Refrigerate until firm. Cover and set remaining gelatin mixture aside at room temperature.
- Meanwhile, combine the cream cheese, Miracle Whip, pecans and celery; spread over chilled gelatin mixture. Carefully pour remaining gelatin mixture over cream cheese layer. Chill overnight.

Nutrition Information

- Calories:
- Total Fat: g
- Cholesterol: mg
- Sodium: mg

- Total Carbohydrate: g
- Protein: g
- Fiber: g

40.Cinnamon Gelatin Salad

Crunchy apples and pecans contrast nicely with smooth gelatin in this pretty salad. --Denita DeValcourt, Lawrenceburg, Tennessee

Serving: 6 servings. | Prep: 15 m | Cook: 0 m | Ready in: 15 m

Ingredients

- 1/4 cup red-hot candies
- 1/4 cup water
- 1 package (6 ounces) raspberry or cherry gelatin
- 1-3/4 cups boiling water
- 1/2 to 1 teaspoon ground cinnamon
- 1-3/4 cups cold water
- 1 medium tart apple, peeled and chopped
- 1/4 cup chopped pecans

Direction

- In a heavy saucepan, cook and stir candies and water until candies are melted. In a bowl, dissolve gelatin in boiling water. Stir in candy mixture and cinnamon. Stir in cold water. Cover and refrigerate until partially set. Fold in apple and pecans. Pour into a 1-1/2-qt. serving bowl. Refrigerate until set.

Nutrition Information

- Calories:
- Total Fat: g
- Cholesterol: mg
- Sodium: mg
- Total Carbohydrate: g
- Protein: g
- Fiber: g

41. Circus Peanut Gelatin

Circus Peanuts were one of the most talked-about candies in my hometown's old-fashioned candy shop. When I saw this gelatin recipe that called for Circus Peanuts, I knew just where to buy them and tried the recipe. Kids love its cool fruity taste, and older folks enjoy the trip down memory lane. -Ruthanne Mengel, Demotte, Indiana

Serving: 12 servings. | Prep: 10 m | Cook: 0 m | Ready in: 10 m

Ingredients

- 44 circus peanut candies, divided
- 1 cup boiling water, divided
- 2 packages (3 ounces each) orange gelatin
- 2 cans (8 ounces each) crushed pineapple, undrained
- 1 carton (8 ounces) frozen whipped topping, thawed

Direction

- Cut 32 candies into small pieces; place in a microwave-safe bowl. Add 1/4 cup of boiling water. Cover and microwave on high for 45 seconds; stir. Microwave 45 seconds longer. Stir until smooth. In a large bowl, dissolve gelatin in remaining boiling water. Stir in candy mixture and pineapple. Refrigerate until partially set.
- Fold in whipped topping. Pour into a 13-in. x 9-in. dish coated with cooking spray. Refrigerate until firm. Cut into squares; top each square with a circus peanut.

Nutrition Information

- Calories: 189 calories
- Total Fat: 3g
- Cholesterol: 0 mg
- Sodium: 16mg
- Total Carbohydrate: 38g
- Protein: 1g
- Fiber: 0 g

42. Citrus Chiffon Salad

Crushed pineapple and orange juice, with a hint of lemon, give this creamy gelatin salad a pleasant tang. The cool fluffy side dish, shared by Kathy Newman of Cedarburg, Wisconsin, is sure to win raves at your next church luncheon.

Serving: 8 servings. | Prep: 10 m | Cook: 0 m | Ready in: 10 m

Ingredients

- 1 cup orange juice
- 1 tablespoon lemon juice
- 1 package (.3 ounce) sugar-free lemon or orange gelatin
- 1 package (8 ounces) fat-free cream cheese, cubed
- 1 cup reduced-fat whipped topping
- 1 can (8 ounces) unsweetened crushed pineapple, undrained
- 1/3 cup reduced-fat mayonnaise

Direction

- In a small saucepan, bring orange and lemon juices to a boil; stir in gelatin until dissolved. In a blender, process the cream cheese, whipped topping, pineapple and mayonnaise until smooth. Add gelatin mixture; cover and process until blended.
- Pour into a 4-cup mold coated with cooking spray. Refrigerate for several hours or overnight until firm.

Nutrition Information

- Calories: 153 calories
- Total Fat: 9g
- Cholesterol: 19mg
- Sodium: 193mg
- Total Carbohydrate: 12g
- Protein: 4g
- Fiber: 0 g

43. Citrus Gelatin Salad

With its sunny color and refreshing citrus flavor, this pretty salad is perfect for summer get-togethers. "This is the only gelatin salad my husband really likes," says Cynthia Norris of Winnetka, California.

Serving: 16 servings. | Prep: 30 m | Cook: 0 m | Ready in: 30 m

Ingredients

- 2 envelopes unflavored gelatin
- 1/4 cup cold water
- 1 cup sugar
- 1-3/4 cups boiling water
- 3 tablespoons lemon juice
- 1 drop yellow food coloring, optional
- 1 can (20 ounces) unsweetened pineapple tidbits, drained
- 1/2 cup sliced firm banana
- 1-1/2 cups miniature marshmallows
- TOPPING:
- 1/2 cup sugar
- 3 tablespoons cornstarch
- 2/3 cup orange juice
- 1/4 cup lemon juice
- 1-1/2 cups reduced-fat whipped topping

Direction

- In a bowl, combine gelatin and cold water; let stand for 1 minute. Add sugar and boiling water; stir until sugar and gelatin are dissolved. Stir in lemon juice and food coloring if desired; set aside. Layer pineapple, banana and marshmallows in a 13-in. x 9-in. dish. Pour gelatin mixture over top. Cover and refrigerate overnight.
- In a saucepan, combine sugar and cornstarch. Gradually stir in juices until smooth. Bring to a boil; cook and stir for 2 minutes or until thickened. Remove from the heat; cool to room temperature. Transfer to a bowl; add whipped topping. Beat until blended. Spread over gelatin layer. Cover and chill for 1 hour or until serving. Cut into squares.

Nutrition Information

- Calories: 132 calories
- Total Fat: 1g
- Cholesterol: 0 mg
- Sodium: 5mg
- Total Carbohydrate: 31g
- Protein: 1g
- Fiber: 0 g

44. Cool Cucumber Salad

This Salad is a refreshing complement to any meal, and it's attractive on the table. Whenever I'm asked to bring a dish to a potluck dinner, I prepare this salad. I often make it for friends and neighbors, too. It's always much appreciated. -- Elisabeth Garrison, Elmer, New Jersey

Serving: 6 servings. | Prep: 20 m | Cook: 0 m | Ready in: 20 m

Ingredients

- 1 medium cucumber
- 1 package (3 ounces) lime gelatin
- 1 teaspoon salt
- 1/2 cup boiling water
- 1 cup mayonnaise
- 1 cup (8 ounces) 4% cottage cheese
- 1 small onion, grated
- Sliced cucumbers and fresh parsley, optional

Direction

- Peel and halve cucumber; remove the seeds. Shred and pat dry; set aside. In a bowl, combine gelatin and salt with boiling water; stir until dissolved. Add mayonnaise and cottage cheese; mix well. Stir in the onion and shredded cucumber. Pour into an oiled 5-cup mold. Refrigerate until firm. Unmold onto a serving platter. Garnish with cucumbers and parsley if desired.

Nutrition Information

- Calories: 370 calories
- Total Fat: 31g
- Cholesterol: 22mg

- Sodium: 759mg
- Total Carbohydrate: 16g
- Protein: 6g
- Fiber: 1g

45. Cool Lime Salad

I've made this recipe for many years. Since my husband is diabetic, one-portion recipes work out well for us.--Elnora Johnson, Union City, Tennessee

Serving: 1 serving. | Prep: 20 m | Cook: 0 m | Ready in: 20 m

Ingredients

- 1/2 cup undrained canned crushed pineapple
- 2 tablespoons lime gelatin
- 1/4 cup 4% cottage cheese
- 1/4 cup whipped topping

Direction

- In a small saucepan, bring pineapple to a boil. Remove from the heat and stir in gelatin until dissolved. Cool to room temperature. Stir in cottage cheese and whipped topping. Chill until set.

Nutrition Information

- Calories: 312 calories
- Total Fat: 6g
- Cholesterol: 13mg
- Sodium: 266mg
- Total Carbohydrate: 57g
- Protein: 10g
- Fiber: 1g

46. Cottage Cheese Fluff

Canned fruit and packaged gelatin are the convenient keys to this dish. It's not your ordinary salad. You can vary the flavor of gelatin or the type of fruits to suit your family's tastes.--Annette Self, Junction City, Ohio

Serving: 8 servings. | Prep: 5 m | Cook: 0 m | Ready in: 5 m

Ingredients

- 1 cup (8 ounces) 4% cottage cheese
- 1 package (3 ounces) gelatin flavor of your choice
- 1 can (11 ounces) mandarin oranges, drained
- 1 cup unsweetened crushed pineapple, drained
- 1/2 cup chopped pecans, optional
- 1 carton (8 ounces) frozen whipped topping, thawed

Direction

- In a large bowl, combine cottage cheese and gelatin powder. Stir in the oranges, pineapple and pecans if desired. Just before serving, fold in the whipped topping.

Nutrition Information

- Calories: 120 calories
- Total Fat: 4g
- Cholesterol: 2mg
- Sodium: 124mg
- Total Carbohydrate: 16g
- Protein: 5g
- Fiber: 0 g

47. Cranberry Cherry Salad

I like to make this refreshing salad for summer get-togethers. It's also a great side dish during the Thanksgiving and Christmas seasons. Everybody just loves it! -Betsy Bianco, Wheaton, Missouri

Serving: 10 servings. | Prep: 20 m | Cook: 0 m | Ready in: 20 m

Ingredients

- 1 can (14-1/2 ounces) pitted tart red cherries
- 1 package (3 ounces) cherry gelatin
- 1 can (8 ounces) jellied cranberry sauce
- 1 package (3 ounces) lemon gelatin
- 1 cup boiling water
- 3 ounces cream cheese, softened
- 1/3 cup mayonnaise
- 1 can (8 ounces) crushed pineapple, undrained
- 1/2 cup heavy whipping cream, whipped
- 1 cup miniature marshmallows

Direction

- Drain cherries, reserving juice; set cherries aside. Add water to juice to measure 1 cup; transfer to a saucepan. Bring to a boil. Add cherry gelatin; stir until dissolved. Whisk in cranberry sauce until smooth. Add cherries; pour into an 11x7-in. dish. Refrigerate until firm.
- In a bowl, dissolve lemon gelatin in boiling water. In a small bowl, beat the cream cheese and mayonnaise. Gradually beat in lemon gelatin until smooth. Stir in pineapple.
- Refrigerate until almost set. Fold in whipped cream and marshmallows. Spoon over cherry layer. Refrigerate until firm.

Nutrition Information

- Calories: 279 calories
- Total Fat: 13g
- Cholesterol: 28mg
- Sodium: 119mg
- Total Carbohydrate: 39g
- Protein: 3g
- Fiber: 1g

48. Cranberry Eggnog Salad

For a bright salad with a vintage holiday feel, we stack a layer of raspberry gelatin and cranberry sauce over pineapple and eggnog. --Nancy Foust, Stoneboro, Pennsylvania

Serving: 12 servings. | Prep: 10 m | Cook: 5 m | Ready in: 15 m

Ingredients

- 2-1/2 cups boiling water
- 2 packages (3 ounces each) cranberry or raspberry gelatin
- 1 can (14 ounces) whole-berry cranberry sauce
- 1 can (20 ounces) crushed pineapple, undrained
- 2 envelopes unflavored gelatin
- 1-1/2 cups eggnog
- 2 tablespoons lime juice

Direction

- In a large bowl, add boiling water to cranberry gelatin; stir 2 minutes to completely dissolve. Refrigerate 40-50 minutes or until slightly thickened.
- Place cranberry sauce in a small bowl; stir to break up. Fold into gelatin mixture. Pour into an 8-cup ring mold coated with cooking spray; refrigerate 15-20 minutes longer or until set but not firm.
- Meanwhile, drain crushed pineapple well, reserving juice in a small saucepan. Sprinkle unflavored gelatin over pineapple juice; let stand 1 minute. Heat and stir over low heat until gelatin is completely dissolved. Stir in eggnog and lime juice. Refrigerate 12-15 minutes or until slightly thickened.
- Fold pineapple into eggnog mixture. Carefully pour over gelatin in mold. Refrigerate until firm. Unmold onto a platter.

Nutrition Information

- Calories: 180 calories
- Total Fat: 1g
- Cholesterol: 19mg
- Sodium: 66mg
- Total Carbohydrate: 37g
- Protein: 7g
- Fiber: 1g

49. Cranberry Gelatin Mold

Tangy and fruity, this festive gelatin mold is not only easy to prepare but pretty, too. Once they've tried it, your family will request it again and again.

Serving: 8 servings. | Prep: 15 m | Cook: 0 m | Ready in: 15 m

Ingredients

- 2 packages (3 ounces each) raspberry gelatin
- 3 cups boiling water
- 1 can (14 ounces) whole-berry cranberry sauce
- 2 tablespoons lemon juice
- 1 can (8 ounces) unsweetened crushed pineapple, drained
- 1/2 cup finely chopped celery

Direction

- In a large bowl, dissolve gelatin in boiling water. Stir in cranberry sauce and lemon juice until blended. Chill until partially set.
- Stir in pineapple and celery. Pour into a 6-cup ring mold coated with cooking spray. Refrigerate until firm. Unmold onto a serving platter.

Nutrition Information

- Calories: 174 calories
- Total Fat: 0 g
- Cholesterol: 0 mg
- Sodium: 479mg
- Total Carbohydrate: 33g
- Protein: 12g
- Fiber: 1g

- Fiber: g

50. Cranberry Gelatin Salad Mold

"Cranberries add tang to this whipped gelatin salad,"
comments field editor Bobbie Talbott of Veneta, Oregon.

Serving: 10-12 servings. | Prep: 20 m | Cook: 0 m |
Ready in: 20 m

Ingredients

- 1 package (12 ounces) cranberries
- 3/4 cup plus 2 tablespoons sugar, divided
- 1-1/2 cups water, divided
- 3/4 cup pineapple tidbits, drained
- 1 medium tart apple, peeled and diced
- 1/4 cup chopped walnuts
- 1 envelope unflavored gelatin
- 1/4 teaspoon salt
- 1/2 cup mayonnaise
- 2 tablespoons lemon juice
- 1 teaspoon grated lemon zest

Direction

- In a saucepan, combine the cranberries, 3/4 cup sugar and 1/2 cup water. Bring to a boil; boil for 3-4 minutes or until berries pop. Remove from the heat; stir in pineapple, apple and nuts. Chill until cooled.
- Place gelatin and remaining water in another saucepan; let stand for 1 minute. Add salt and remaining sugar; cook and stir over low heat until dissolved. Remove from the heat; stir in the mayonnaise, lemon juice and zest.
- Transfer to a bowl; chill until partially set, about 1 hour. Beat until fluffy. Fold in cranberry mixture. Pour into a 6-cup mold coated with cooking spray. Chill until firm, about 8 hours.

Nutrition Information

- Calories:
- Total Fat: g
- Cholesterol: mg
- Sodium: mg
- Total Carbohydrate: g
- Protein: g

51. Cranberry Gelatin Squares

This festive gelatin treat from Lucile Cline of Wichita, Kansas is full of cranberries, pineapple and pecans. It's a great recipe to serve on the holiday buffet table.

Serving: 12 servings. | Prep: 30 m | Cook: 0 m | Ready in: 30 m

Ingredients

- 2 cans (8 ounces each) crushed pineapple
- 2 packages (3 ounces each) strawberry gelatin
- 3/4 cup cold water
- 1 can (14 ounces) jellied cranberry sauce
- 1/3 cup chopped pecans
- 1 tablespoon butter
- 1/2 cup cold whole milk
- 1/2 cup heavy whipping cream
- 1 package (3.4 ounces) instant vanilla pudding mix
- 3 ounces cream cheese, softened

Direction

- Preheat oven to 350 degrees. Drain pineapple, reserving juice in a 1-cup measuring cup. Add enough water to measure 1 cup. Set pineapple aside.
- In a small saucepan over medium heat, bring pineapple juice mixture to a boil. Remove from the heat; stir in gelatin until dissolved. Stir in cold water; transfer to a bowl. Cover and refrigerate until partially set.
- In a small bowl, combine cranberry sauce and reserved pineapple; stir into gelatin mixture. Pour into a 9-in. square dish; cover and refrigerate until firm.
- Place pecans and butter in a shallow baking pan. Bake 8 minutes or until golden brown, stirring occasionally; cool.
- In a small bowl, whisk milk, cream and pudding mix 2 minutes. In another small bowl, beat cream cheese until smooth. Add pudding mixture; beat on low speed just until

combined. Spread over gelatin. Sprinkle with toasted pecans. Chill until firm.

Nutrition Information

- Calories: 255 calories
- Total Fat: 10g
- Cholesterol: 25mg
- Sodium: 189mg
- Total Carbohydrate: 41g
- Protein: 3g
- Fiber: 1g

52. Cranberry Luncheon Salad

In the heart of cranberry country, Mrs. Leon F. Schleusener, Tomah, Wisconsin, has key ingredients for her salad at hand. If you can't find cranberry gelatin, raspberry or other red-colored flavors work, too.

Serving: 10 servings. | Prep: 25 m | Cook: 0 m | Ready in: 25 m

Ingredients

- 2 cups orange juice, divided
- 1 cup water
- 2 packages (3 ounces each) cranberry gelatin
- 1 can (14 ounces) whole-berry cranberry sauce
- 1 can (15-1/4 ounces) sliced peaches, drained
- 3 cups cubed cooked chicken
- 2 celery ribs, chopped
- 1/2 cup mayonnaise
- 1 tablespoon cider vinegar
- 1/2 teaspoon salt
- 1/8 teaspoon pepper
- Lettuce leaves
- 1/4 cup coarsely chopped pecans

Direction

- In a small saucepan, bring 1 cup orange juice and water to a boil. Place gelatin in a large bowl; add juice mixture and stir until dissolved. Stir in the remaining orange juice. Chill until partially set, about 1-1/2 hours.

- Stir in cranberry sauce. Pour into a 6-cup ring mold coated with cooking spray. Cover and refrigerate for 6 hours or overnight.
- Set aside a few peach slices for garnish; cube the remaining peaches. In a large bowl, combine the cubed peaches, chicken, celery, mayonnaise, vinegar, salt and pepper. Cover and refrigerate for 1 hour or until chilled.
- Invert gelatin mold onto a serving plate; line center of ring with lettuce leaves. Stir pecans into chicken salad; spoon into center of gelatin. Top with reserved peach slices.

Nutrition Information

- Calories:
- Total Fat: g
- Cholesterol: mg
- Sodium: mg
- Total Carbohydrate: g
- Protein: g
- Fiber: g

53. Cranberry Pecan Salad

We harvest close to 500,000 pounds of pecans on our land here in West Texas. So, of course, I use pecans in many recipes. This tasty, colorful salad is great for holiday gatherings.--Janice Rogers, Odessa, Texas

Serving: 12-16 servings. | Prep: 10 m | Cook: 0 m | Ready in: 10 m

Ingredients

- 3 packages (3 ounces each) orange gelatin
- 3 cups boiling water
- 2-1/2 cups fresh or frozen cranberries
- 1-1/2 cups finely chopped celery
- 2 oranges, peeled, sectioned and diced
- 1 can (8 ounces) crushed pineapple, undrained
- 2 tablespoons grated orange zest
- 1 cup sugar
- 2 tablespoons lemon juice
- Dash salt
- 3/4 cup chopped pecans

Direction

- In a bowl, dissolve gelatin in boiling water. Stir in cranberries, celery, oranges, pineapple with liquid, orange zest, sugar, lemon juice and salt. Chill until partially set. Stir in pecans. Pour into 8-cup mold. Chill until firm.

Nutrition Information

- Calories: 132 calories
- Total Fat: 4g
- Cholesterol: 0 mg
- Sodium: 32mg
- Total Carbohydrate: 24g
- Protein: 1g
- Fiber: 2g

54. Cranberry Relish Salad

SO MUCH time and effort went into preparing meals for our large family that it was a real bonus to find a recipe with a shortcut. This salad was one of them. The dish became part of a special meal our family enjoyed during the holidays. I recall lots of second helpings being requested, but not many leftovers. -Rosemary Talcott, Worthington, Minnesota

Serving: 12 servings. | Prep: 10 m | Cook: 0 m | Ready in: 10 m

Ingredients

- 1 package (3 ounces) cherry gelatin
- 1 package (3 ounces) raspberry gelatin
- 1/4 cup sugar
- 1-1/2 cups boiling water
- 1 can (12 ounces) lemon-lime soda
- 1 can (8 ounce) crushed pineapple, undrained
- 2 packages (10 ounces each) frozen cranberry-orange sauce

Direction

- In a large bowl, dissolve the gelatins and sugar in boiling water. Add the soda, pineapple and cranberry-orange sauce; chill until partially set. Pour into individual dishes or an 11x7-in. dish. Refrigerate overnight or until firm.

Nutrition Information

- Calories: 133 calories
- Total Fat: 0 g
- Cholesterol: 0 mg
- Sodium: 43mg
- Total Carbohydrate: 33g
- Protein: 1g
- Fiber: 0 g

55. Cranberry Salad

"CRANBERRIES seem to be traditional with everyone's Thanksgiving meal in one form or another. This salad is our favorite way to serve them, either as an attractive mold or for individual salads. The nuts and other fruit give it a refreshing crunch."

Serving: 12-15 servings. | Prep: 20 m | Cook: 0 m | Ready in: 20 m

Ingredients

- 1 cup sugar
- 1 cup water
- 1 package (6 ounces) lemon gelatin
- 4 cups fresh cranberries, finely chopped
- 2 large unpeeled apples, finely chopped
- 1 unpeeled orange, seeded and finely chopped
- 1/2 cup chopped pecans
- Lettuce leaves, optional
- Mayonnaise, optional

Direction

- In a large saucepan, bring sugar and water to a boil, stirring constantly. Remove from the heat; immediately stir in gelatin until dissolved. Chill until mixture is the consistency of unbeaten egg whites.
- Fold in the cranberries, apples, orange and pecans. Spoon into greased individual salad molds, a 6-1/2-cup ring mold or an 11x7-in. dish. Chill until firm. If desired, serve on lettuce leaves and top with a dollop of mayonnaise.

Nutrition Information

- Calories: 147 calories
- Total Fat: 3g
- Cholesterol: 0 mg
- Sodium: 26mg
- Total Carbohydrate: 31g
- Protein: 2g
- Fiber: 2g

Nutrition Information

- Calories: 275 calories
- Total Fat: 6g
- Cholesterol: 0 mg
- Sodium: 3mg
- Total Carbohydrate: 55g
- Protein: 4g
- Fiber: 4g

56. Cranberry Salad Mold

"THERE WAS always a cranberry salad on our holiday table#151;Mother made it with fresh raw cranberries. I was delighted when she would ask me to help grind the cranberries in her old food grinder...I could go on turning its crank forever. How I loved hearing the cranberries pop as they passed through!"

Serving: 12 servings. | Prep: 30 m | Cook: 0 m | Ready in: 30 m

Ingredients

- 8 cups fresh cranberries
- 2-1/2 cups sugar
- 2 tablespoons unflavored gelatin
- 1/3 cup orange juice
- 2 cups diced apples
- 1 cup chopped nuts
- Leaf lettuce and mayonnaise for garnish

Direction

- Finely grind the cranberries in a food chopper. Add sugar and mix thoroughly. Let stand 15 minutes, stirring occasionally. (If using frozen berries, let them stand until the mixture is at room temperature.) Place the gelatin and orange juice in the top of a double boiler; stir over hot water until gelatin is dissolved. Add to cranberries along with apples and nuts; place in a 7-cup mold that has been rinsed in cold water. Chill until set. Unmold onto leaf lettuce. Garnish with mayonnaise.

57. Cranberry Turkey Salad

This recipe is most treasured because it's from my husband's grandmother. A savory turkey salad is cleverly topped with cranberry-raspberry gelatin for an eye-catching dish. --Kim Kirven, Wadsworth, Ohio

Serving: 12-15 servings. | Prep: 20 m | Cook: 0 m | Ready in: 20 m

Ingredients

- 1 package (3 ounces) lemon gelatin
- 2 cups boiling water, divided
- 2 cups cubed cooked turkey or chicken
- 4 celery ribs, chopped
- 8 ounces process cheese (Velveeta), cubed
- 1 cup chopped almonds
- 3 hard-boiled large eggs, chopped, optional
- 1 cup Miracle Whip
- 1 cup heavy whipping cream, whipped
- 1/2 teaspoon salt
- 1/2 teaspoon onion salt
- 1 package (3 ounces) raspberry gelatin
- 1 can (14 ounces) whole-berry cranberry sauce

Direction

- In a bowl, dissolve lemon gelatin in 1 cup of boiling water; refrigerate for 1 hour or until slightly thickened. Beat for 1 minute on high speed. Stir in turkey, celery, cheese, almonds, eggs if desired, Miracle Whip, cream, salt and onion salt. Spread evenly into a 13-in. x 9-in. dish. Cover and refrigerate until firm, about 2 hours.

- Dissolve the raspberry gelatin in remaining boiling water; stir in cranberry sauce until melted and blended. Spoon over turkey mixture. Refrigerate for 2 hours or until set. Cut into squares.

Nutrition Information

- Calories: 379 calories
- Total Fat: 27g
- Cholesterol: 51mg
- Sodium: 460mg
- Total Carbohydrate: 25g
- Protein: 12g
- Fiber: 2g

58. Cranberry Waldorf Gelatin

We enjoy this easy-to-make salad in the fall when apples are in season. Their crisp freshness adds so much to a favorite dish. — Debbie Short, Carlisle, Iowa

Serving: 12 servings. | Prep: 15 m | Cook: 0 m | Ready in: 15 m

Ingredients

- 1 envelope unflavored gelatin
- 1 cup cold water, divided
- 1 package (3 ounces) cranberry gelatin
- 2 cups boiling water
- 1 can (14 ounces) whole-berry cranberry sauce
- 1/2 to 1 teaspoon ground cinnamon
- 1/4 teaspoon ground ginger
- 1/8 to 1/4 teaspoon salt
- 2 medium tart apples, peeled and diced
- 1 cup chopped walnuts

Direction

- Sprinkle unflavored gelatin over 1/4 cup cold water; let stand for 5 minutes. In a bowl, dissolve softened gelatin and cranberry gelatin in boiling water. Stir in cranberry sauce until blended. Add the cinnamon, ginger, salt and remaining cold water. Cover and refrigerate until almost set. Fold in apples and walnuts.

Pour into an ungreased 2-1/2-qt. serving bowl. Refrigerate until firm.

Nutrition Information

- Calories: 156 calories
- Total Fat: 6g
- Cholesterol: 0 mg
- Sodium: 50mg
- Total Carbohydrate: 24g
- Protein: 4g
- Fiber: 1g

59. Cranberry Eggnog Gelatin Salad

Refreshing and bursting with flavor, this festive salad is a great choice for a holiday potluck. The sweet pineapple-eggnog layer contrasts nicely with the cool and tangy gelatin on top. Since it has to chill overnight, it's a good pick for those dishes you want to prepare a day ahead. — Nancy Foust, Stoneboro, Pennsylvania

Serving: 16 servings. | Prep: 30 m | Cook: 5 m | Ready in: 35 m

Ingredients

- 2 packages (3 ounces each) raspberry gelatin
- 2 cups boiling water
- 1 cup cold water
- 1 can (14 ounces) whole-berry cranberry sauce
- 1 medium navel orange, peeled and chopped
- 1 tablespoon grated orange zest
- 1 can (20 ounces) unsweetened crushed pineapple, undrained
- 2 envelopes unflavored gelatin
- 1-1/2 cups eggnog
- 3 tablespoons lime juice

Direction

- In a large bowl, dissolve raspberry gelatin in boiling water. Stir in cold water, then cranberry sauce, orange and orange zest. Pour into a 10-in. fluted tube pan or 12-cup ring mold coated with cooking spray; refrigerate for 40 minutes or until firm.

- Meanwhile, drain pineapple; pour juice into a saucepan. Sprinkle unflavored gelatin over juice and let stand for 1 minute. Cook and stir over low heat until gelatin is completely dissolved.
- In a large bowl, combine eggnog and lime juice. Gradually stir in gelatin mixture. Chill until soft-set. Fold in pineapple. Spoon over raspberry layer. Refrigerate overnight. Unmold onto a serving platter.

Nutrition Information

- Calories:
- Total Fat: g
- Cholesterol: mg
- Sodium: mg
- Total Carbohydrate: g
- Protein: g
- Fiber: g

60. CranberryOrange Molded Salad

This colorful side dish will complement virtually any meal. The cinnamon and cloves combined with the cranberry sauce and orange sections give this salad an interesting, zesty taste. It's particularly nice at holidays, when its bright color adds a festive touch to your table!

Serving: 8-10 servings. | Prep: 10 m | Cook: 0 m | Ready in: 10 m

Ingredients

- 1 package (6 ounces) raspberry gelatin
- 2 cups boiling water
- 1 can (14 ounces) whole-berry cranberry sauce
- 1/4 teaspoon ground cinnamon
- Dash ground cloves
- 2 cups diced orange sections
- Lettuce leaves, optional

Direction

- In a large bowl, dissolve gelatin in boiling water. Stir in cranberry sauce, cinnamon and cloves. Chill until partially set. Add the orange sections. Pour into an oiled 6-cup mold. Chill until set, about 3 hours. Unmold; serve on a lettuce-lined platter if desired.

Nutrition Information

- Calories: 144 calories
- Total Fat: 0 g
- Cholesterol: 0 mg
- Sodium: 48mg
- Total Carbohydrate: 36g
- Protein: 2g
- Fiber: 2g

61. CranberryPineapple Gelatin Mold

This cranberry mold has become a tradition in our home during the holidays. You can use a blender to combine the cranberries and oranges if you don't have a food processor.
--Bethany Ring, Conneaut, Ohio

Serving: 10 servings. | Prep: 15 m | Cook: 5 m | Ready in: 20 m

Ingredients

- 1 can (20 ounces) unsweetened crushed pineapple
- 2 envelopes unflavored gelatin
- 1 package (12 ounces) fresh or frozen cranberries
- 3 medium navel oranges, peeled and cut into segments
- 1/2 cup honey
- Whipped cream, optional

Direction

- Drain pineapple, reserving juice; set pineapple aside. Place reserved juice in a small saucepan. Sprinkle with gelatin; let stand for 1 minute or until softened. Heat over low heat, stirring until gelatin is completely dissolved. Remove from the heat.

- In a food processor, combine cranberries and oranges; cover and pulse until chunky. Add honey and pineapple; cover and pulse just until blended. Stir in juice mixture. Transfer to a 6-cup mold coated with cooking spray. Refrigerate until firm.
- Unmold onto a serving platter. Serve with whipped cream if desired.

Nutrition Information

- Calories: 126 calories
- Total Fat: 0 g
- Cholesterol: 0 mg
- Sodium: 5mg
- Total Carbohydrate: 32g
- Protein: 2g
- Fiber: 3g

62. CranBlueberry Mold

"I found this not-too-sweet recipe in our local newspaper many years ago. It's a family favorite--especially when fresh blueberries are in season," shares Cindy Steffen from Cedarburg, Wisconsin.

Serving: 6 servings. | Prep: 20 m | Cook: 0 m | Ready in: 20 m

Ingredients

- 2 envelopes unflavored gelatin
- 1-1/2 cups cold water
- Sugar substitute equivalent to 1/4 cup sugar
- 2 cups reduced-calorie reduced-sugar cranberry juice, chilled
- 2 cups fresh peaches, peeled and cut into chunks
- 1-1/2 cups fresh blueberries

Direction

- In a saucepan, sprinkle gelatin over water; let stand for 1 minute. Add sugar substitute.

Cook and stir until mixture is warm and gelatin and sugar substitute are dissolved (do not boil). Transfer to a bowl. Stir in cranberry juice. Cover and refrigerate until slightly thickened. Fold in peaches and blueberries. Transfer to a 7-cup mold or 2-qt. bowl coated with cooking spray. Refrigerate until firm. Unmold onto a plate or serving platter.

Nutrition Information

- Calories: 71 calories
- Total Fat: 0 g
- Cholesterol: 0 mg
- Sodium: 9mg
- Total Carbohydrate: 16g
- Protein: 3g
- Fiber: 2g

63. CranOrange Gelatin Salad

After seeing this gelatin salad in a flier, I decided to make it lighter. I like to serve it as a fruit salad, but others may like it for a sweet treat. --Eva DeWolf, Erwin, Tennessee

Serving: 15 servings. | Prep: 45 m | Cook: 0 m | Ready in: 45 m

Ingredients

- 1 can (15 ounces) mandarin oranges
- 2 packages (.3 ounce each) sugar-free cranberry gelatin
- 1-1/2 cups boiling water
- 1 can (14 ounces) whole-berry cranberry sauce
- 1-1/2 cups crushed salt-free pretzels
- 6 tablespoons butter, melted
- Sugar substitute equivalent to 5 tablespoons sugar, divided
- 1 package (8 ounces) fat-free cream cheese
- 1 carton (8 ounces) frozen reduced-fat whipped topping, thawed

Direction

- Drain oranges, reserving juice in a 2-cup measuring cup; set oranges and juice aside.

- In a large bowl, dissolve gelatin in boiling water. Stir in cranberry sauce until melted. Add enough cold water to the reserved juice to measure 1-1/2 cups; add to gelatin mixture. Stir in oranges. Chill until partially set.
- Meanwhile, in a large bowl, combine the pretzels, butter and 2 tablespoons sugar substitute. Press into an ungreased 13-in. x 9-in. dish; chill.
- In a small bowl, beat cream cheese and remaining sugar substitute until smooth. Fold in whipped topping. Spread over crust. Spoon gelatin mixture over cream cheese layer. Chill for at least 3 hours or until set.

Nutrition Information

- Calories: 183 calories
- Total Fat: 7g
- Cholesterol: 13mg
- Sodium: 185mg
- Total Carbohydrate: 26g
- Protein: 4g
- Fiber: 1g

64. CranRaspberry Gelatin

You'll love the sweet-tart flavor and beautiful ruby-red color of this chunky fruit salad from Katy Jarvis of Bear Creek, Wisconsin. "It's great served with a Thanksgiving turkey or with most any kind of meat," she writes.

Serving: 8 servings. | Prep: 15 m | Cook: 0 m | Ready in: 15 m

Ingredients

- 1 package (3 ounces) raspberry gelatin
- 1-1/2 cups boiling water
- 1 cup fresh cranberries or frozen cranberries
- 1/2 cup raspberry jam or spreadable fruit
- 1 can (8 ounces) crushed pineapple, undrained

Direction

- In a bowl, dissolve gelatin in water. Place cranberries, jam and gelatin mixture in a blender or food processor; cover and process until cranberries are coarsely chopped. Transfer to a bowl; stir in pineapple. Refrigerate until set.

Nutrition Information

- Calories: 58 calories
- Total Fat: 1g
- Cholesterol: 0 mg
- Sodium: 30mg
- Total Carbohydrate: 14g
- Protein: 1g
- Fiber: 0 g

65. CranRaspberry Gelatin Salad

Just like Grandma's, this pretty gelatin salad has full berry flavor without being too tart. It's perfect for Thanksgiving dinner.

Serving: 10 servings. | Prep: 15 m | Cook: 0 m | Ready in: 15 m

Ingredients

- 2 packages (3 ounces each) raspberry gelatin
- 1 cup boiling water
- 1 can (14 ounces) whole-berry cranberry sauce
- 1 can (8 ounces) crushed pineapple, undrained
- 1 cup orange juice

Direction

- In a large bowl, dissolve gelatin in boiling water. Stir in the cranberry sauce, pineapple and orange juice. Pour into a 6-cup ring mold coated with cooking spray.
- Cover and refrigerate for 4 hours or until set. Unmold onto a serving platter.

Nutrition Information

- Calories: 155 calories
- Total Fat: 0 g
- Cholesterol: 0 mg
- Sodium: 49mg

- Total Carbohydrate: 39g
- Protein: 2g
- Fiber: 1g

66. CranRaspberry Sherbet Mold

Folks who love the flavor of raspberries and cranberries rave about this tart molded gelatin salad. It's easy to make and pretty enough for company and festive occasions. I like to garnish it with whole cranberries and raspberries. - Judith Outlaw, Washougal, Washington

Serving: 10-12 servings. | Prep: 10 m | Cook: 0 m | Ready in: 10 m

Ingredients

- 2 packages (3 ounces each) raspberry gelatin
- 1-1/2 cups boiling water
- 1 can (14 ounces) jellied cranberry sauce
- 2 cups raspberry sherbet, softened
- 1 tablespoon lemon juice
- Cranberries, raspberries, orange segments and fresh mint, optional

Direction

- In a large bowl, dissolve gelatin in boiling water. Stir in cranberry sauce until smooth. Refrigerate for 30 minutes or until slightly thickened.
- Fold in sherbet and lemon juice. Transfer to a 6-cup ring mold coated with cooking spray. Refrigerate until firm.
- Unmold onto a serving platter. Fill center with cranberries and raspberries, and serve with oranges and mint if desired.

Nutrition Information

- Calories: 114 calories
- Total Fat: 0 g
- Cholesterol: 1mg
- Sodium: 36mg
- Total Carbohydrate: 28g
- Protein: 1g
- Fiber: 1g

67. Creamy Blueberry Gelatin Salad

Plump blueberries and a fluffy topping star in this pretty, refreshing salad. My mom's blueberry salad was served at every holiday and celebration. Now, my grandchildren look forward to sampling it at holidays. --Sharon Hoefert, Greendale, Wisconsin

Serving: 15 servings. | Prep: 30 m | Cook: 0 m | Ready in: 30 m

Ingredients

- 2 packages (3 ounces each) grape gelatin
- 2 cups boiling water
- 1 can (21 ounces) blueberry pie filling
- 1 can (20 ounces) unsweetened crushed pineapple, undrained
- TOPPING:
- 1 package (8 ounces) cream cheese, softened
- 1 cup sour cream
- 1/2 cup sugar
- 1 teaspoon vanilla extract
- 1/2 cup chopped walnuts

Direction

- In a large bowl, dissolve gelatin in boiling water. Cool for 10 minutes. Stir in pie filling and pineapple until blended. Transfer to a 13x9-in. dish. Cover and refrigerate until partially set, about 1 hour.
- For topping, in a small bowl, combine the cream cheese, sour cream, sugar and vanilla. Carefully spread over gelatin; sprinkle with walnuts. Cover and refrigerate until firm.

Nutrition Information

- Calories: 221 calories
- Total Fat: 10g
- Cholesterol: 27mg
- Sodium: 76mg
- Total Carbohydrate: 29g
- Protein: 4g

- Fiber: 1g

68. Creamy Citrus Salad

This crowd-pleasing salad frequently appeared on the table while I was growing up. But with my four brothers, it never lasted long! The flavors are a nice addition to any meal.

Serving: 12-14 servings. | Prep: 20 m | Cook: 0 m | Ready in: 20 m

Ingredients

- 1 package (6 ounces) orange gelatin
- 2 cups boiling water
- 1 can (6 ounces) frozen orange juice concentrate, thawed
- 2 cans (11 ounces each) mandarin oranges, drained
- 1 can (20 ounces) crushed pineapple, undrained
- 1 cup cold milk
- 1 package (3.4 ounces) instant lemon pudding mix
- 1 cup heavy whipping cream, whipped

Direction

- In a large bowl, dissolve gelatin in boiling water; stir in orange juice concentrate. Cool until partially set. Fold in oranges and pineapple. Pour into a greased 13-in. x 9-in. dish. Chill until firm.
- In a small bowl, beat milk and pudding mix for 2 minutes; fold in cream. Spread over gelatin. Chill for 30 minutes.

Nutrition Information

- Calories: 196 calories
- Total Fat: 7g
- Cholesterol: 26mg
- Sodium: 127mg
- Total Carbohydrate: 33g
- Protein: 3g
- Fiber: 1g

69. Creamy Cranberry Gelatin

Looking for a tasty take-along for holiday potlucks? Consider this colorful contribution from Collette Burch of Edinburg, Texas. The sweet-tart salad can be started the day before your event.

Serving: 10 servings. | Prep: 20 m | Cook: 0 m | Ready in: 20 m

Ingredients

- 1 package (12 ounces) fresh or frozen cranberries, chopped
- 1 to 1-1/4 cups sugar
- 2 packages (3 ounces each) cherry gelatin
- 2 cups (16 ounces) plain yogurt
- 1 carton (8 ounces) frozen whipped topping, thawed
- 1/3 cup chopped pecans

Direction

- In a bowl, combine the cranberries and sugar; cover and refrigerate for 8 hours or overnight.
- In a large saucepan, combine the cranberry mixture and gelatin. Cook and stir until gelatin is completely dissolved; cool. Fold in the yogurt and whipped topping. Pour into a 2-qt. serving bowl. Sprinkle with pecans. Refrigerate for 2 hours or until firm.

Nutrition Information

- Calories: 204 calories
- Total Fat: 6g
- Cholesterol: 1mg
- Sodium: 83mg
- Total Carbohydrate: 33g
- Protein: 4g
- Fiber: 2g

70. Creamy Cranberry Pineapple Gelatin

I picked up this recipe at the gas company when I was a teen in the fifties. I modified it slightly, entered it in a newspaper contest and won $100! It was a delight to our family's taste buds.

Serving: 6 servings. | Prep: 15 m | Cook: 0 m | Ready in: 15 m

Ingredients

- 1 cup orange juice
- 1 package (3 ounces) pineapple gelatin
- 3 ounces cream cheese, softened
- 1 can (14 ounces) jellied cranberry sauce

Direction

- In a small saucepan, bring orange juice to a boil. Place gelatin in a small bowl; add orange juice and stir until dissolved. Refrigerate until slightly thickened.
- In a small bowl, beat cream cheese until fluffy. Add cranberry sauce; beat until smooth. Beat in gelatin mixture. Pour into six 1/2-cup gelatin molds coated with cooking spray. Refrigerate for several hours or overnight. Unmold onto serving plates.

Nutrition Information

- Calories: 227 calories
- Total Fat: 5g
- Cholesterol: 16mg
- Sodium: 90mg
- Total Carbohydrate: 45g
- Protein: 3g
- Fiber: 1g

71. Creamy Fruit Mold

Because it can be made ahead, a gelatin salad like this one, brimming with fruit and nuts, is so convenient. This salad (another old standby from the cooking show I watched years ago) comes out of the mold easily and looks very attractive when served. -Shirley Leister, West Chester, Pennsylvania

Serving: 6 servings. | Prep: 10 m | Cook: 0 m | Ready in: 10 m

Ingredients

- 3 ounces cream cheese, softened
- 1 package (3 ounces) lime gelatin
- 1 cup boiling water
- 1/4 cup mayonnaise
- 1 can (15-1/4 ounces) fruit cocktail, drained
- 1/2 cup chopped pecans

Direction

- In a bowl, beat cream cheese and gelatin. Add water, stir until gelatin is dissolved. Refrigerate until thickened, about 1 hour, stirring frequently. Add mayonnaise; whisk until smooth. Stir in fruit and pecans. Pour into a 1-qt. mold that has been coated with cooking spray. Chill until firm. Unmold onto a serving platter.

Nutrition Information

- Calories: 289 calories
- Total Fat: 19g
- Cholesterol: 19mg
- Sodium: 129mg
- Total Carbohydrate: 28g
- Protein: 4g
- Fiber: 2g

72. Creamy n Fruity Gelatin Salad

I CAN remember looking forward to eating this pretty salad when I was a child. It has all the ingredients a child would like. My Grandmother served it during the holidays and on other special occasions and my Mother did the same.

Serving: 10 servings. | Prep: 15 m | Cook: 0 m | Ready in: 15 m

Ingredients

- 2 packages (3 ounces each) orange gelatin
- 1 cup boiling water
- 1 pint orange or pineapple sherbet
- 1 can (11 ounces) mandarin oranges, drained
- 1 can (8 ounces) crushed pineapple, drained
- 1 cup miniature marshmallows
- 1 cup heavy whipping cream, whipped

Direction

- In a large bowl, dissolve gelatin in boiling water. Add sherbet; stir until smooth. Stir in the oranges, pineapple and marshmallows. Fold in whipped cream.
- Pour into a 6-cup serving bowl. Cover and refrigerate for 3-4 hours or until set.

Nutrition Information

- Calories: 158 calories
- Total Fat: 5g
- Cholesterol: 18mg
- Sodium: 42mg
- Total Carbohydrate: 28g
- Protein: 2g
- Fiber: 0 g

73. Creamy Orange Fluff

I got this yummy recipe from a friend but came up with my own tasty topping. Creamy, fruity and refreshing, this dish is simple to make ahead and cuts nicely into squares for ease in serving. It is perfect for potlucks.

Serving: 15 servings. | Prep: 15 m | Cook: 0 m | Ready in: 15 m

Ingredients

- 1 package (6 ounces) orange gelatin
- 2-1/2 cups boiling water
- 2 cans (11 ounces each) mandarin oranges, drained
- 1 can (8 ounces) crushed pineapple, undrained
- 1 can (6 ounces) frozen orange juice concentrate, thawed
- TOPPING:
- 1 package (8 ounces) cream cheese, softened
- 1 cup cold 2% milk
- 1 package (3.4 ounces) instant vanilla pudding mix

Direction

- In a large bowl, dissolve gelatin in boiling water. Stir in oranges, pineapple and orange juice concentrate. Coat a 13-in. x 9-in. dish with cooking spray; add gelatin mixture. Chill until firm.
- In a large bowl, beat cream cheese until smooth. Gradually add milk and pudding mix; beat until smooth. Spread over orange layer. Chill until firm.

Nutrition Information

- Calories: 181 calories
- Total Fat: 6g
- Cholesterol: 17mg
- Sodium: 125mg
- Total Carbohydrate: 31g
- Protein: 3g
- Fiber: 1g

74. Creamy Orange Gelatin

After celebrating two graduations in less than a year, it was clear that this recipe was definitely everyone's favorite.
--Sue Gronholz, Beaver Dam, Wisconsin

Serving: 12 servings (3/4 cup each). | Prep: 20 m | Cook: 0 m | Ready in: 20 m

Ingredients

- 4 cups boiling water
- 4 packages (3 ounces each) orange gelatin
- 1 quart vanilla ice cream, softened
- 1-1/2 cups orange juice
- 2 cans (11 ounces each) mandarin oranges, drained
- Orange slices, optional

Direction

- Add boiling water to gelatin; stir 2 minutes to completely dissolve. Stir in ice cream and orange juice until blended. Refrigerate until partially set.
- Fold in oranges. Pour into two 6-cup ring molds coated with cooking spray. Refrigerate overnight or until firm. Unmold onto a serving plate. If desired, serve with orange slices.

Nutrition Information

- Calories: 224 calories
- Total Fat: 5g
- Cholesterol: 19mg
- Sodium: 102mg
- Total Carbohydrate: 43g
- Protein: 5g
- Fiber: 0 g

75. Creamy Orange Salad

This cool, light and pretty salad has a refreshing orange taste that complements any big meal. With just five ingredients, it's very simple to prepare. I've served it for my family and shared it at potlucks. - Priscilla Weaver, Hagerstown, Maryland

Serving: 10-12 servings. | Prep: 10 m | Cook: 0 m | Ready in: 10 m

Ingredients

- 1 package (6 ounces) orange gelatin
- 2 cups boiling water
- 2 packages (3 ounces each) cream cheese, softened
- 1 can (14 ounces) sweetened condensed milk
- 1 carton (8 ounces) frozen whipped topping, thawed
- Maraschino cherry, fresh mint stem and mandarin oranges, optional

Direction

- In a bowl, dissolve gelatin in water. In a bowl, beat cream cheese until fluffy. Gradually blend in the hot gelatin mixture, beating on low speed until smooth. Stir in the milk; fold in whipped topping.
- Transfer to a 2-1/2-qt. serving bowl. Refrigerate for 4 hours or until firm. If desired, garnish with a flower made of cherry, mint and oranges.

Nutrition Information

- Calories: 272 calories
- Total Fat: 10g
- Cholesterol: 23mg
- Sodium: 110mg
- Total Carbohydrate: 41g
- Protein: 5g
- Fiber: 0 g

76. Crisp Cranberry Gelatin

How can gelatin be "crisp?" When it's chock-full of chopped apple and celery! This tangy favorite gets a nice crunch from walnuts, too.

Serving: 12 servings. | Prep: 10 m | Cook: 10 m | Ready in: 20 m

Ingredients

- 2 cups fresh or frozen cranberries
- 1-1/2 cups water
- 1 cup sugar
- 1 package (3 ounces) orange gelatin
- 1 medium apple, chopped
- 1 celery rib, chopped
- 1/2 cup chopped walnuts
- 1/4 cup orange juice
- 2 teaspoons grated orange zest

Direction

- In a large saucepan, bring cranberries and water to a boil. Reduce heat; simmer for 3 minutes or until the berries pop, stirring occasionally. Stir in sugar and gelatin until dissolved. Pour into an 11x7-in. dish; refrigerate until set but not firm, about 1 hour.
- Combine the apple, celery, walnuts, orange juice and zest; stir into gelatin mixture. Refrigerate until firm.

Nutrition Information

- Calories:
- Total Fat: g
- Cholesterol: mg
- Sodium: mg
- Total Carbohydrate: g
- Protein: g
- Fiber: g

77. Cucumber Grapefruit Mold

This old-fashioned gelatin is sure to bring back memories of Christmases past. It's a refreshing addition to a heavy meal.

Serving: 6 servings. | Prep: 15 m | Cook: 10 m | Ready in: 25 m

Ingredients

- 3 large pink grapefruit
- 1 envelope unflavored gelatin
- 1/4 cup cold water
- 2 tablespoons sugar
- 1/8 teaspoon salt
- 1 tablespoon white balsamic vinegar
- 1 cup chopped seeded peeled cucumber
- Leaf lettuce leaves, optional

Direction

- Cut each grapefruit in half; remove sections, reserving juice. Set sections aside. Add enough water to juice to measure 1-1/2 cups.
- In a small bowl, sprinkle gelatin over cold water; let stand for 1 minute.
- Meanwhile, in a small saucepan, combine the sugar, salt and grapefruit juice mixture. Cook and stir until sugar is dissolved. Remove from the heat; stir in gelatin until completely dissolved. Stir in vinegar. Chill until slightly thickened, about 1 hour.
- Fold in cucumber and grapefruit sections. Transfer to a 1-qt. mold coated with cooking spray. Refrigerate until firm.
- Unmold onto a lettuce-lined serving plate if desired.

Nutrition Information

- Calories: 77 calories
- Total Fat: 0 g
- Cholesterol: 0 mg
- Sodium: 53mg
- Total Carbohydrate: 19g
- Protein: 2g
- Fiber: 2g

78. Eggnog Molded Salad

For an excellent holiday gelatin salad, try this one. It looks so lovely on a platter and tastes good with the fruit and a hint of eggnog flavor. It goes well with any meal because it's refreshing. -Alice Ceresa, Rochester, New York

Serving: 12 servings. | Prep: 35 m | Cook: 0 m | Ready in: 35 m

Ingredients

- 1 teaspoon unflavored gelatin
- 1 can (15-1/4 ounces) sliced pears
- 1 package (6 ounces) lemon gelatin
- 1 cup sour cream
- 3/4 cup eggnog
- 1 can (11 ounces) mandarin oranges, drained
- Orange slices, maraschino cherries and mint leaves, optional

Direction

- In a small bowl, sprinkle unflavored gelatin over 1/4 cup cold water; let stand 1 minute.
- Drain pears over a 2-cup measuring cup, reserving syrup. Add enough water to the syrup to measure 2 cups; pour into a saucepan. Bring to a boil; remove from heat. Add lemon gelatin and unflavored gelatin mixture; stir 2 minutes to dissolve completely. Cool 15 minutes.
- Stir in sour cream and eggnog until well blended. Refrigerate until partially set.
- Cut oranges and drained pears into chunks; stir into gelatin mixture. Pour into a 6-cup ring mold coated with cooking spray. Refrigerate, covered, until firm. If desired, serve with oranges, cherries and mint.

Nutrition Information

- Calories:
- Total Fat: g
- Cholesterol: mg
- Sodium: mg
- Total Carbohydrate: g
- Protein: g
- Fiber: g

79. Festive Fruit Gelatin

"I use this during the holidays because of the color combination, but it's good anytime!" With cranberry sauce, pineapple and cream cheese, there's a wonderful variety of flavors in this recipe. Barbara Knapp - Bennington, Vermont

Serving: 12 servings. | Prep: 15 m | Cook: 0 m | Ready in: 15 m

Ingredients

- 1 package (.3 ounce) sugar-free lime gelatin
- 3 cups boiling water, divided
- 1 can (8 ounces) unsweetened crushed pineapple, undrained
- 1-1/2 teaspoons unflavored gelatin
- 2 tablespoons cold water
- 1 package (8 ounces) reduced-fat cream cheese
- 1/4 cup fat-free milk
- 2 packages (.3 ounce each) sugar-free strawberry gelatin
- 1 can (14 ounces) jellied cranberry sauce

Direction

- In a small bowl, dissolve lime gelatin in 1 cup boiling water; stir in pineapple. Pour into a 13-in. x 9-in. dish coated with cooking spray. Refrigerate until set but not firm.
- Sprinkle gelatin over cold water; let stand for 1 minute. Microwave on high for 15 seconds. Stir and let stand for 1 minute or until gelatin is completely dissolved.
- In a small bowl, beat cream cheese until fluffy. Gradually add milk and gelatin mixture; beat until smooth. Gently spread over lime layer. Refrigerate until set but not firm.
- In a large bowl, dissolve strawberry gelatin in remaining boiling water. Whisk in cranberry sauce until smooth. Refrigerate until partially set. Gently spread over cream cheese layer. Refrigerate until firm.

Nutrition Information

- Calories: 122 calories
- Total Fat: 4g
- Cholesterol: 13mg
- Sodium: 139mg
- Total Carbohydrate: 18g
- Protein: 4g
- Fiber: 1g

Nutrition Information

- Calories: 193 calories
- Total Fat: 4g
- Cholesterol: 0 mg
- Sodium: 66mg
- Total Carbohydrate: 33g
- Protein: 3g
- Fiber: 2g

---

80. Flavorful Cranberry Gelatin Mold

A little port or Merlot wine offers a tasty twist to this traditional gelatin that also features pineapple and walnuts. I make it for holiday dinners, especially when turkey or ham is served. --Jenice Gibson of Oregon City, Oregon

Serving: 8 servings. | Prep: 10 m | Cook: 0 m | Ready in: 10 m

Ingredients

- 2 packages (.3 ounce each) sugar-free raspberry gelatin
- 1-1/2 cups boiling water
- 1 can (20 ounces) unsweetened crushed pineapple, drained
- 1 can (14 ounces) whole-berry cranberry sauce
- 1/2 cup chopped walnuts
- 1/3 cup port wine or red grape juice
- Mint leaves for garnish, optional

Direction

- In a large bowl, dissolve gelatin in boiling water. Stir in the pineapple, cranberry sauce, walnuts and wine.
- Pour into a 5-cup mold coated with cooking spray. Run a knife through the gelatin mixture to evenly distribute the fruit. Refrigerate 2-1/2 hours or until firm.
- Unmold onto a serving plate. Garnish with mint if desired.

---

81. Fluffy Cranberry Delight

This was originally my daughter's recipe, and she or I will make it for one or more of our holiday get-togethers. It can be served as a fruit salad along with the meal or as a light dessert. It's particularly pretty in a cut-glass bowl on a buffet. --Ruth Bolduc, Conway, New Hampshire

Serving: 8-10 servings. | Prep: 20 m | Cook: 0 m | Ready in: 20 m

Ingredients

- 4 cups cranberries
- 1-1/2 cups sugar
- 3/4 cup water
- 1 envelope unflavored gelatin
- 1/4 cup lemon juice
- 2 tablespoons orange juice
- 1-1/2 cups heavy whipping cream
- 3 tablespoons confectioners' sugar
- 1 teaspoon vanilla extract

Direction

- In a saucepan, bring the cranberries, sugar and water to a boil. Reduce heat and cook until berries burst. Strain through a food mill or sieve into a large bowl.
- Stir in the gelatin, lemon juice and orange juice. Cool until mixture coats the back of a spoon.
- In a small bowl, whip cream until soft peaks form. Add confectioners' sugar and vanilla; beat until stiff peaks form. Fold into cranberry mixture. Chill until set.

Nutrition Information

- Calories: 273 calories
- Total Fat: 13g
- Cholesterol: 49mg
- Sodium: 16mg
- Total Carbohydrate: 39g
- Protein: 2g
- Fiber: 2g

- Cholesterol: 16mg
- Sodium: 37mg
- Total Carbohydrate: 22g
- Protein: 2g
- Fiber: 1g

82. Fluffy Cranberry Mousse

This is a delicious and pretty salad for the holidays, but it's so good that I serve it at other times, too. I got the recipe from a neighbor who had served it with a traditional turkey dinner. --Helen Clement, Hemet, California

Serving: 16-20 servings. | Prep: 15 m | Cook: 0 m | Ready in: 15 m

Ingredients

- 1 package (6 ounces) strawberry gelatin
- 1 cup boiling water
- 1 can (20 ounces) crushed pineapple
- 1 can (14 ounces) whole-berry cranberry sauce
- 3 tablespoons lemon juice
- 1 teaspoon grated lemon zest
- 1/2 teaspoon ground nutmeg
- 2 cups sour cream
- 1/2 cup chopped pecans

Direction

- In a large bowl, dissolve gelatin in boiling water. Drain pineapple, setting the pineapple aside and adding juice to gelatin. Stir in cranberry sauce, lemon juice, zest and nutmeg. Chill until mixture thickens. Fold in sour cream, pineapple and pecans. Pour into a glass serving bowl or an oiled 9-cup mold. Chill until set, at least 2 hours.

Nutrition Information

- Calories: 150 calories
- Total Fat: 6g

83. Fluffy Lime Salad

Crunchy walnuts, plump marshmallows and tangy pineapple dot this creamy lime salad. It's a refreshing side dish for a family meal or a yummy addition to a potluck dinner. -Susan Ormond, Jamestown, North Carolina

Serving: 9 servings. | Prep: 15 m | Cook: 0 m | Ready in: 15 m

Ingredients

- 1 can (8 ounces) crushed pineapple
- 1 package (3 ounces) lime gelatin
- 3 tablespoons water
- 2 packages (3 ounces each) cream cheese, softened
- 1 cup chopped walnuts
- 1 cup miniature marshmallows
- 1 cup heavy whipping cream, whipped

Direction

- Drain pineapple, reserving juice; set the pineapple aside. In a saucepan, combine gelatin, water and reserved juice. Cook and stir over low heat until gelatin is dissolved. Refrigerate until syrupy, about 30 minutes.
- In a small bowl, beat cream cheese until fluffy. Stir in gelatin mixture, walnuts, marshmallows and reserved pineapple. Fold in the whipped cream.
- Transfer to a 1-qt. serving bowl. Cover and refrigerate for 2 hours or until set.

Nutrition Information

- Calories: 276 calories
- Total Fat: 21g
- Cholesterol: 47mg
- Sodium: 63mg

- Total Carbohydrate: 19g
- Protein: 6g
- Fiber: 1g

84. Fluffy Raspberry Salad

I've modified this recipe slightly since I first served it for Thanksgiving dinner many years ago. It's always a hit.-- Teresa Shattuck, Oak Park, Illinois

Serving: 32-40 servings. | Prep: 10 m | Cook: 0 m | Ready in: 10 m

Ingredients

- 3 packages (3 ounces each) raspberry gelatin
- 2 packages (3 ounces each) orange gelatin
- 5 cups boiling water
- 4 packages (10 ounces each) frozen sweetened raspberries
- 1 jar (20 ounces) chunky applesauce
- 3 cups miniature marshmallows
- 2 cups heavy whipping cream, whipped

Direction

- Dissolve gelatin in boiling water. Add raspberries; stir until thawed. Stir in applesauce. Refrigerate until partially set.
- Fold in the marshmallows and whipped cream. Pour into two 13-in. x 9-in. dishes. Refrigerate until firm.

Nutrition Information

- Calories: 87 calories
- Total Fat: 4g
- Cholesterol: 16mg
- Sodium: 16mg
- Total Carbohydrate: 12g
- Protein: 1g
- Fiber: 0 g

85. For Goodness Sakes Salad

I've shared this salad recipe more than any other in file. Upon reading the list of ingredients, folks often exclaim, "Well, for goodness sakes!"...hence the name! The unusual blend of flavors makes this one of our family's favorite.

Serving: 12-16 servings. | Prep: 15 m | Cook: 0 m | Ready in: 15 m

Ingredients

- 1 package (3 ounces) lemon gelatin
- 1 package (3 ounces) lime gelatin
- 1 cup boiling water
- 1 cup evaporated milk
- 1 can (20 ounces) crushed pineapple, undrained
- 1 cup mayonnaise
- 1 cup (8 ounces) 4% cottage cheese
- 1 cup chopped nuts
- 1 tablespoon horseradish sauce

Direction

- In a large bowl, dissolve the gelatins in boiling water. Cool slightly. Stir in the milk, pineapple with juice, mayonnaise, cottage cheese, nuts and horseradish sauce; mix well. Chill until partially set. Pour into an oiled 8-cup mold. Chill for 6 hours or overnight. Unmold.

Nutrition Information

- Calories: 252 calories
- Total Fat: 17g
- Cholesterol: 14mg
- Sodium: 171mg
- Total Carbohydrate: 20g
- Protein: 6g
- Fiber: 1g

86. Fourth of July JellO

"With six children, I'm always looking for wholesome quick recipes," shares Mabel Yoder of Bonduel, Wisconsin. "This colorful salad can be fixed by school-age children and looks so pretty served in a glass bowl."

Serving: 6-8 servings. | Prep: 15 m | Cook: 0 m | Ready in: 15 m

Ingredients

- 1 package (3 ounces) berry blue gelatin
- 2 cups boiling water, divided
- 1/2 cup cold water, divided
- 1 package (3 ounces) strawberry gelatin
- 1 can (15 ounces) pear halves, drained and cubed

Direction

- In a large bowl, dissolve the berry gelatin in 1 cup boiling water. Stir in 1/4 cup cold water. Pour into an ungreased 9x5-in. loaf pan. Refrigerate until firm. Repeat with strawberry gelatin and remaining boiling and cold water.
- When gelatin is set, cut into cubes. Just before serving, gently combine gelatin cubes and pears in a large glass bowl or individual dishes.

Nutrition Information

- Calories: 117 calories
- Total Fat: 0 g
- Cholesterol: 0 mg
- Sodium: 51mg
- Total Carbohydrate: 29g
- Protein: 2g
- Fiber: 1g

87. Frankenstein Salads

Kids of all ages will love these fun and fruity Frankenstein faces made from rectangles of jiggly green gelatin resting on bright purple kale. Bean sprout hair, jelly bean eyes and nose, mini marshmallow bolts and a sour cream smile give this memorable monster some playful personality.

Serving: 6 servings. | Prep: 20 m | Cook: 0 m | Ready in: 20 m

Ingredients

- 2 packages (6 ounces each) lime gelatin
- 2-1/2 cups boiling water
- 3/4 cup bean sprouts
- 12 orange jelly beans
- 6 red jelly beans
- 3 tablespoons sour cream
- 12 miniature marshmallows
- Purple kale, optional

Direction

- In a bowl, dissolve gelatin in water. Pour into an 8-in. square pan that has been coated with cooking spray. Refrigerate for 4 hours or until firm. Cut into six rectangles; place each on a plate. Decorate with bean sprouts for hair, orange jelly beans for eyes and a red jelly bean for nose. Fill a small plastic bag with sour cream; cut a small hole in the corner of the bag. Pipe a jagged smile on face. Place marshmallows on side of head for bolts. Garnish plates with kale if desired.

Nutrition Information

- Calories:
- Total Fat: g
- Cholesterol: mg
- Sodium: mg
- Total Carbohydrate: g
- Protein: g
- Fiber: g

88. Frosted Cranberry Gelatin Salad

Covered with a fluffy white topping, squares of this fruity gelatin salad can be served as a side dish or dessert.

Serving: 9-12 servings. | Prep: 20 m | Cook: 10 m | Ready in: 30 m

Ingredients

- 1 can (8 ounces) crushed pineapple
- 2 packages (3 ounces each) lemon gelatin
- 1 cup ginger ale, chilled
- 1 can (14 ounces) jellied cranberry sauce
- 1/2 cup chopped peeled tart apple
- 1/2 cup chopped celery
- 1 package (8 ounces) cream cheese, softened
- 1/4 cup sugar
- 1 envelope whipped topping mix (Dream Whip)
- 1/2 cup chopped pecans, toasted

Direction

- Drain pineapple, reserving juice; set pineapple aside. Add enough water to juice to measure 1 cup. Pour into a small saucepan; bring to a boil. Carefully pour into a large bowl; stir in gelatin until dissolved. Add ginger ale. Refrigerate until syrupy, about 45 minutes.
- Combine the cranberry sauce, apple, celery and reserved pineapple; fold into gelatin mixture. Transfer to a 9-in. square dish. Refrigerate until firm.
- In a small bowl, beat cream cheese and sugar until fluffy. Prepare whipped topping mix according to package directions; fork into cream cheese mixture. Spread over gelatin. Sprinkle with pecans.

Nutrition Information

- Calories: 265 calories
- Total Fat: 11g
- Cholesterol: 21mg
- Sodium: 102mg
- Total Carbohydrate: 41g
- Protein: 3g
- Fiber: 1g

89. Frosted Cranberry Salad

--Carolyn Sellers, York, Pennsylvania

Serving: 8 servings. | Prep: 30 m | Cook: 0 m | Ready in: 30 m

Ingredients

- 1 can (20 ounces) crushed pineapple
- 1 envelope unflavored gelatin
- 1 package (3 ounces) cherry gelatin
- 1 cup chilled ginger ale
- 1 can (14 ounces) jellied cranberry sauce
- 1 package (8 ounces) cream cheese, softened
- 1 envelope whipped topping mix (Dream Whip)
- 1/2 cup milk
- 1 teaspoon vanilla extract
- 8 pecan halves, toasted
- 8 fresh cranberries

Direction

- Drain pineapple, reserving juice in a 1 cup measure; set pineapple aside. To the juice, add enough water to measure 1 cup. Transfer to a small saucepan; add the unflavored gelatin and let stand for 1 minute. Bring to a boil. Add cherry gelatin; stir until dissolved. Stir in ginger ale. Pour into a bowl. Refrigerate for 30 minutes or until partially set.
- Whisk in the pineapple and cranberry sauce. Transfer to an 11x7-in. dish coated with cooking spray. Refrigerate until set.
- In a large bowl, beat cream cheese until smooth. In a small bowl, beat whipped topping mix, milk and vanilla on low speed until blended. Beat on high for 4 minutes or until thickened. Add to cream cheese; beat until blended. Spread over gelatin. Refrigerate overnight. Cut into squares; garnish each with a pecan half and cranberry.

Nutrition Information

- Calories:
- Total Fat: g

51

- Cholesterol: mg
- Sodium: mg
- Total Carbohydrate: g
- Protein: g
- Fiber: g

- Cholesterol: 3mg
- Sodium: 191mg
- Total Carbohydrate: 25g
- Protein: 6g
- Fiber: 1g

90. Frosted Fruit Gelatin Salad

Shares field editor Sherry Hulsman of Louisville, Kentucky, "I often take this fruity salad to potlucks and other gatherings. With its fluffy topping, it's always popular."

Serving: 9 servings. | Prep: 20 m | Cook: 0 m | Ready in: 20 m

Ingredients

- 1 can (15 ounces) blueberries
- 1 can (8 ounces) unsweetened pineapple tidbits
- 1 package (.6 ounce) sugar-free raspberry gelatin
- 2 cups boiling water
- 1 package (8 ounces) fat-free cream cheese, softened
- 1/2 cup fat-free sour cream
- 1/3 cup sugar
- 1/2 teaspoon vanilla extract

Direction

- Drain blueberries and pineapple, reserving juice; set fruit aside. In a bowl, dissolve gelatin in boiling water. Add enough water to reserved fruit juices to measure 1-1/4 cups; stir into gelatin. Chill until partially set. Stir in reserved fruit. Pour into an 8-in. square dish. Refrigerate until firm.
- In a bowl, combine cream cheese and sour cream. Beat in sugar and vanilla. Carefully spread over the gelatin. Refrigerate until serving.

Nutrition Information

- Calories: 125 calories
- Total Fat: 1g

91. Frosted Gelatin Salad

A sweet, creamy topping frosts tis extra-fruity gelatin that is chock-full of canned apricots and crushed pineapple. "It's a colorful salad to serve at potluck dinners," reports Bertha Johnson of Indianapolis, Indiana. "Everyone loves the combination of flavors."

Serving: 12 servings. | Prep: 20 m | Cook: 0 m | Ready in: 20 m

Ingredients

- 2 packages (3 ounces each) orange gelatin
- 2 cups boiling water
- 3/4 cup miniature marshmallows
- 2 cans (15-1/4 ounces each) apricot halves
- 1 can (20 ounces) crushed pineapple, drained
- 1/2 cup sugar
- 3 tablespoons all-purpose flour
- 1 egg, lightly beaten
- 1 teaspoon vanilla extract
- 2 envelopes whipped topping mix (Dream Whip)
- 1/4 cup finely shredded cheddar cheese

Direction

- In a large bowl, dissolve gelatin in boiling water. Add marshmallows; stir until melted. Drain apricots, reserving 1 cup juice; set juice aside. Chop apricots; add to gelatin with pineapple. Pour into an 11x7-in. dish. Chill until firm.
- Meanwhile, in a small saucepan, combine the sugar and flour. Whisk in the egg, vanilla and reserved apricot juice until smooth. Bring to a boil; boil and stir for 2 minutes. Cool completely.
- Prepare whipped topping according to package directions; fold in cooled juice

mixture. Spread over gelatin. Sprinkle with cheese. Chill for 1 hour.

Nutrition Information

- Calories:
- Total Fat: g
- Cholesterol: mg
- Sodium: mg
- Total Carbohydrate: g
- Protein: g
- Fiber: g

92. Frosted Orange Salad

Pineapple, bananas and marshmallows are folded into orange Jell-O in this refreshing salad. Frosted with a creamy topping, pecans and coconut, this yummy dish is a real crowd-pleaser. I have been making it for years. -Anna Jean Key, Muskogee, Oklahoma

Serving: 12 servings. | Prep: 35 m | Cook: 0 m | Ready in: 35 m

Ingredients

- 3 packages (3 ounces each) orange gelatin
- 3 cups boiling water
- 1 can (20 ounces) crushed pineapple
- 3 cups cold water
- 4 medium firm bananas, sliced
- 2-1/2 cups miniature marshmallows
- 1/2 cup sugar
- 1 tablespoon all-purpose flour
- 1 egg, lightly beaten
- 1 package (8 ounces) cream cheese, softened
- 1 cup heavy whipping cream, whipped
- 3/4 cup chopped pecans, toasted
- 1/2 cup sweetened shredded coconut, toasted

Direction

- In a large bowl, dissolve gelatin in boiling water. Drain pineapple, reserving juice. Stir the cold water, bananas, marshmallows and pineapple into gelatin.

- Pour into a 13-in. x 9-in. dish coated with cooking spray; refrigerate until firm.
- Meanwhile, in a large saucepan, combine sugar and flour. Stir in reserved pineapple juice until smooth. Bring to a boil over medium heat; cook and stir for 2 minutes or until thickened and bubbly. Reduce heat; cook and stir 2 minutes longer.
- Remove from the heat. Stir a small amount of hot filling into the egg; return all to the pan, stirring constantly. Bring to a gentle boil; cook and stir 2 minutes longer. Cool.
- In a large bowl, beat cream cheese until smooth. Beat in, cooled filling. Fold in whipped cream. Spread over gelatin (dish will be full). Sprinkle with nuts and coconut.

Nutrition Information

- Calories: 369 calories
- Total Fat: 21g
- Cholesterol: 66mg
- Sodium: 101mg
- Total Carbohydrate: 44g
- Protein: 5g
- Fiber: 2g

93. Frosted Pineapple Lemon Gelatin

A refreshing, summery treat, this dessert incorporates ginger ale to add a zesty bite. --Penny Burpeau, Londonderry, New Hampshire

Serving: 12 servings. | Prep: 20 m | Cook: 10 m | Ready in: 30 m

Ingredients

- 1 can (20 ounces) crushed pineapple
- 2 packages (3 ounces each) lemon gelatin
- 2 cups boiling water
- 2 cups ginger ale, chilled
- 2 large firm bananas, sliced
- 1/2 cup sugar
- 2 tablespoons all-purpose flour

- 1 large egg, lightly beaten
- 2 tablespoons butter
- 1 cup heavy whipping cream

Direction

- Drain pineapple, reserving juice; set pineapple aside. In a large bowl, dissolve gelatin in boiling water. Stir in the ginger ale, bananas and crushed pineapple. Transfer to a 13x9-in. dish. Refrigerate until firm.
- For topping, combine sugar and flour in a small saucepan. Gradually whisk in reserved pineapple juice. Bring to a boil over medium heat; cook and stir for 2 minutes or until thickened.
- Remove from the heat. Stir a small amount into egg; return all to the pan, stirring constantly. Cook and stir until a thermometer reads 160 degrees and mixture is thickened. Remove from the heat; stir in butter. Cool to room temperature.
- In a small bowl, beat cream on high speed until stiff peaks form. Gently fold into custard. Spread over gelatin. Refrigerate for 1 hour or until chilled.

Nutrition Information

- Calories: 250 calories
- Total Fat: 10g
- Cholesterol: 50mg
- Sodium: 63mg
- Total Carbohydrate: 40g
- Protein: 3g
- Fiber: 1g

94. Frosted Strawberry Salad

My daughter, Katherine Beth, has requested that her grandmother, Thelma Bell, make this sweet rick gelatin salad with its fluffy topping for every family get-together. So when she and Patrick Althouse planned their nuptials, this delightful salad was part of the bountiful potluck buffet.

Serving: 16-20 servings. | Prep: 15 m | Cook: 0 m | Ready in: 15 m

Ingredients

- 2 packages (6 ounces each) strawberry gelatin
- 3 cups boiling water
- 2 packages (10 ounces each) frozen sweetened sliced strawberries, thawed
- 1 can (20 ounces) crushed pineapple, undrained
- 1 cup chopped pecans
- 1/2 cup chopped maraschino cherries
- TOPPING:
- 1 package (8 ounces) cream cheese, softened
- 1 jar (7 ounces) marshmallow creme
- 1 carton (8 ounces) frozen whipped topping, thawed
- Fresh strawberries and mint

Direction

- In a large bowl, dissolve gelatin in boiling water. Stir in strawberries and pineapple. Refrigerate until partially set.
- Stir in pecans and cherries. Transfer to a 13-in. x 9-in. dish. Chill for 2 hours or until firm.
- For topping, in a small bowl, beat cream cheese and marshmallow creme just until combined; fold in whipped topping. Spread over salad. Chill for several hours or overnight. Cut into squares. Garnish with strawberries and mint.

Nutrition Information

- Calories: 216 calories
- Total Fat: 10g
- Cholesterol: 12mg
- Sodium: 65mg
- Total Carbohydrate: 30g

- Protein: 2g
- Fiber: 1g

95. Fruit Parfaits

These parfaits are a refreshing fruity treat, and you can use whatever flavor of gelatin you like. Because it calls for canned fruit, you can rely on it as a tasty dessert anytime of year.--Erlene Cornelius, Spring City, Tennessee

Serving: 4 servings. | Prep: 25 m | Cook: 0 m | Ready in: 25 m

Ingredients

- 1 can (15 ounces) fruit cocktail
- 1 package (3 ounces) lemon gelatin
- 8 ice cubes (1-1/2 cups crushed ice)

Direction

- Drain fruit cocktail, reserving syrup. Divide fruit among four parfait glasses and set aside. Add water to the syrup to measure 3/4 cup; pour into a saucepan. Bring to a boil.
- Place gelatin in a blender; carefully add syrup. Cover and blend on low until gelatin is dissolved, about 30 seconds. Add ice; cover and blend until dissolved, about 1 minute. Pour over the fruit. Cover and refrigerate until set, about 15 minutes.

Nutrition Information

- Calories: 69 calories
- Total Fat: 0 g
- Cholesterol: 0 mg
- Sodium: 53mg
- Total Carbohydrate: 16g
- Protein: 1g
- Fiber: 0 g

96. Fruited Cranberry Gelatin

"A neighbor gave my mom this recipe, and it's become an annual favorite during the holidays," relates field editor Linda Fox of Soldotna, Alaska.

Serving: 12-16 servings. | Prep: 20 m | Cook: 0 m | Ready in: 20 m

Ingredients

- 1 package (6 ounces) cranberry or raspberry gelatin
- 1/2 cup sugar
- 1-1/2 cups boiling water
- 1 package (12 ounces) cranberries
- 3 medium unpeeled green apples, cut into wedges
- 1 medium navel orange, peeled and quartered
- 1 cup diced celery
- 1 cup chopped pecans
- 1 cup cold water
- 1 tablespoon cider vinegar
- 2 teaspoons grated orange zest
- 1-1/2 teaspoons lemon juice
- 1/2 teaspoon salt
- 3/4 cup mayonnaise
- 2 tablespoons orange juice

Direction

- In a large bowl, dissolve gelatin and sugar in boiling water. In a blender or food processor, process the cranberries until coarsely chopped; add to gelatin mixture. Repeat with apples and orange. Stir in celery, pecans, water, vinegar, orange zest, lemon juice and salt. Pour into a 13x9-in. dish or a 2-1/2-qt. bowl. Chill until set, about 3 hours.
- Whisk mayonnaise and orange juice; serve with the salad.

Nutrition Information

- Calories: 221 calories
- Total Fat: 14g
- Cholesterol: 4mg
- Sodium: 161mg
- Total Carbohydrate: 25g
- Protein: 2g

- Fiber: 3g

97. Fruited Cranberry Salad

Whenever we have a special-occasion family gathering, I'm always asked to bring along this cool and fruity salad. Everyone loves the combination of tart cranberries and sweet oranges, grapes and pineapple.--Edna Havens, Wann, Oklahoma

Serving: 12 servings. | Prep: 45 m | Cook: 0 m | Ready in: 45 m

Ingredients

- 2 cups fresh or frozen cranberries
- 1 medium unpeeled orange, cut into wedges and seeds removed
- Sugar substitute equivalent to 3/4 cup sugar
- 1 package (.3 ounce) sugar-free cherry gelatin
- 1 cup boiling water
- 1 cup seedless red grapes, halved
- 1 cup unsweetened crushed pineapple, drained
- 1/2 cup diced celery
- 1/4 cup finely chopped pecans

Direction

- In a blender or food processor, combine the first three ingredients. Cover and process until the fruit is coarsely chopped; let stand for 30 minutes.
- Meanwhile, in a large bowl, dissolve gelatin in water. Refrigerate for 15-20 minutes or until mixture begins to thicken. Add cranberry mixture, grapes, pineapple, celery and pecans. Pour into a 2-qt. serving bowl or individual dishes. Refrigerate for several hours or overnight.

Nutrition Information

- Calories: 49 calories
- Total Fat: 2g
- Cholesterol: 0 mg
- Sodium: 5mg
- Total Carbohydrate: 9g
- Protein: 1g

- Fiber: 0 g

98. Fruited Gelatin Salad

I've found this salad to be perfect for potlucks and special occasions. It cuts nicely into squares and can be served on lettuce leaves if you like. --Norma Warner, Hot Springs Village, Arkansas

Serving: 12-16 servings. | Prep: 30 m | Cook: 0 m | Ready in: 30 m

Ingredients

- 2 packages (3 ounces each) orange gelatin
- 2 cups boiling water
- 1 cup apricot nectar
- 1 cup pineapple juice
- 1 can (15 ounces) apricot halves, drained and mashed
- 1 can (8 ounces) crushed pineapple, drained
- 4 cups miniature marshmallows
- TOPPING:
- 1/2 cup sugar
- 2 tablespoons all-purpose flour
- 1/2 cup apricot nectar
- 1/2 cup pineapple juice
- 1 large egg, lightly beaten
- 2 tablespoons butter
- 1 cup heavy whipping cream
- 1 cup shredded cheddar cheese

Direction

- In a large bowl, dissolve gelatin in boiling water. Stir in the juices, apricots and pineapple. Transfer to a 13x9-in. dish coated with cooking spray. Refrigerate for 30 minutes or until partially set. Sprinkle with marshmallows; refrigerate.
- For topping, combine sugar and flour in a saucepan. Gradually whisk in juices. Bring to a boil over medium heat; cook and stir for 2 minutes or until thickened. Removed from the heat. Stir a small amount into egg; return all to the pan, stirring constantly. Cook and stir until a thermometer reads 160 degrees and mixture

is thickened. Remove from the heat; stir in butter. Cool to room temperature.

- In a small bowl, beat cream on high speed until stiff peaks form. Gently fold into custard. Spread over gelatin; sprinkle with cheese. Refrigerate 1 hour or until chilled.

Nutrition Information

- Calories: 242 calories
- Total Fat: 10g
- Cholesterol: 46mg
- Sodium: 91mg
- Total Carbohydrate: 38g
- Protein: 4g
- Fiber: 1g

99. Fruited Lemon Gelatin Salad

As light and pleasant as a summer breeze - that's how I would describe this sunny salad. With oranges, grapes and pineapple peeking out of every spoonful, it's a fun, fruity addition to any meal. -Erla Burkholder, Ewing, Illinois

Serving: 15-18 servings. | Prep: 30 m | Cook: 0 m | Ready in: 30 m

Ingredients

- 1 package (6 ounces) lemon gelatin
- 2 cups boiling water
- 1 can (12 ounces) lemon-lime soda
- 1 can (20 ounces) crushed pineapple
- 1 can (15 ounces) mandarin oranges, drained
- 2 cups halved green grapes
- 1 egg
- 1/2 cup sugar
- 2 tablespoons all-purpose flour
- 1 tablespoon butter
- 1 cup heavy whipping cream, whipped
- Lettuce leaves, optional

Direction

- Dissolve gelatin in boiling water. Stir in soda. Chill until partially set.

- Drain pineapple, reserving juice; set pineapple aside. Add water to pineapple juice, if necessary, to measure 1 cup; set aside. Stir the pineapple, oranges and grapes into gelatin. Pour into a greased 13-in. x 9-in. dish. Chill until firm.
- Meanwhile, in a large saucepan over medium heat, combine the egg, sugar, flour, butter and reserved pineapple juice. Bring to a boil; cook and stir for 2 minutes or until thickened. Cool completely. Fold in whipped cream. Spread over gelatin. Chill until firm. Cut into squares; serve on lettuce if desired.

Nutrition Information

- Calories: 146 calories
- Total Fat: 4g
- Cholesterol: 23mg
- Sodium: 38mg
- Total Carbohydrate: 29g
- Protein: 2g
- Fiber: 1g

100. FruitFilled Raspberry Ring

People love this fruity gelatin ring that gets extra flavor from an ambrosia-like mixture in the center. I've been bringing it to potlucks, buffets and showers for 20 years. While it looks like you fussed, it's easy to make the night before a special occasion. -Janice Steinmetz, Somers, Connecticut

Serving: 12-16 servings. | Prep: 10 m | Cook: 0 m | Ready in: 10 m

Ingredients

- 2 packages (6 ounces each) raspberry gelatin
- 4 cups boiling water
- 1 quart raspberry sherbet
- 1 can (14 ounces) pineapple tidbits, drained
- 1 can (11 ounces) mandarin oranges, drained
- 1 cup sweetened shredded coconut
- 1 cup miniature marshmallows
- 1 cup (8 ounces) sour cream

Direction

- In a large bowl, dissolve gelatin in boiling water. Stir in sherbet until melted. Pour into an 8-cup ring mold coated with cooking spray. Chill overnight or until firm.
- In another large bowl, combine the pineapple, oranges, coconut, marshmallows and sour cream. Cover and chill. To serve, unmold gelatin onto a serving plate. Spoon fruit mixture into center of ring.

Nutrition Information

- Calories: 180 calories
- Total Fat: 5g
- Cholesterol: 12mg
- Sodium: 68mg
- Total Carbohydrate: 32g
- Protein: 2g
- Fiber: 1g

101. FruitPacked Gelatin Salad

A rich creamy layer makes this fruity gelatin stand out from the rest. "I always get comments as well as requests for the recipe," comments Linda Kaufman of Columbus, Ohio. Loaded with berry, pineapple and banana flavors, it is perfect for potlucks.

Serving: 15 servings. | Prep: 20 m | Cook: 0 m | Ready in: 20 m

Ingredients

- 2 packages (.3 ounce each) sugar-free strawberry gelatin
- 2 cups boiling water
- 2 packages (12 ounces each) frozen unsweetened strawberries, thawed and cut in half
- 1 can (20 ounces) unsweetened crushed pineapple
- 3 medium firm bananas, sliced
- 1 package (8 ounces) reduced-fat cream cheese
- 1 cup fat-free sour cream
- 1/2 cup chopped walnuts, toasted

Direction

- In a large bowl, dissolve gelatin in boiling water. Stir in the strawberries, pineapple and bananas. Transfer to a 13-in. x 9-in. dish coated with cooking spray. Cover and refrigerate for about 1 hour or until partially set.
- In a small bowl, combine the cream cheese and sour cream until blended. Carefully spread over gelatin mixture. Cover and refrigerate until firm. Just before serving, sprinkle with walnuts.

Nutrition Information

- Calories: 142 calories
- Total Fat: 6g
- Cholesterol: 13mg
- Sodium: 105mg
- Total Carbohydrate: 19g
- Protein: 5g
- Fiber: 2g

102. Fruity Gelatin Salad

This pretty side dish is ideal for big holiday dinners. It's refreshing, sweet and tart and has just the right amount of tang.--Sarah Baumann, Saginaw, Texas

Serving: 36-40 servings. | Prep: 15 m | Cook: 0 m | Ready in: 15 m

Ingredients

- 2 packages (6 ounces each) cherry gelatin
- 2 cups boiling water
- 2 packages (10 ounces each) frozen sweetened sliced strawberries
- 2 cans (20 ounces each) crushed pineapple, undrained
- 2 cans (16 ounces each) whole-berry cranberry sauce

Direction

- In two large bowls, dissolve gelatin in boiling water. Stir in strawberries until berries are separated. Stir in the pineapple and cranberry sauce until blended. Transfer to two 13-in. x 9-in. dishes. Refrigerate until firm.

Nutrition Information

- Calories: 47 calories
- Total Fat: 0 g
- Cholesterol: 0 mg
- Sodium: 12mg
- Total Carbohydrate: 12g
- Protein: 0 g
- Fiber: 0 g

103. Fruity Lime Salad Mold

A DEAR FRIEND shared this recipe with me over 30 years ago, and it has appeared on our table frequently all these years. It's rich tasting, plus the touch of red maraschino cherries makes it a real treat for the holidays or any special occasion. -Jean Kirkland, Newport, Oregon

Serving: 6-8 servings. | Prep: 10 m | Cook: 0 m | Ready in: 10 m

Ingredients

- 1 package (3 ounces) lime gelatin
- 1 cup boiling water
- 3 ounces cream cheese, softened
- 1 can (8 ounces) crushed pineapple, undrained
- 1 cup heavy whipping cream, whipped
- 1/4 cup chopped pecans
- 1/4 cup chopped maraschino cherries

Direction

- In a large bowl, dissolve gelatin in boiling water; chill until syrupy. In a small bowl, combine cream cheese and pineapple; stir into cooled gelatin.
- Fold in whipped cream, pecans and cherries. Pour into a 4-cup mold coated with cooking spray. Refrigerate for 3 hours or overnight.

Nutrition Information

- Calories:
- Total Fat: g
- Cholesterol: mg

- Sodium: mg
- Total Carbohydrate: g
- Protein: g
- Fiber: g

104. Fruity Orange Gelatin

Pineapple and oranges add sweet fruit flavor to this attractive salad from Esther Miller of Holmesville, Ohio. "The addition of sherbet makes this gelatin especially refreshing," she adds. "It's quick to prepare ahead of time and keep in the refrigerator until serving."

Serving: 10-12 servings. | Prep: 20 m | Cook: 0 m | Ready in: 20 m

Ingredients

- 1 package (6 ounces) orange gelatin
- 2 cups boiling water
- 2 cups orange sherbet
- 1 can (20 ounces) crushed pineapple, undrained
- 1 can (11 ounces) mandarin oranges, drained

Direction

- In a bowl, dissolve gelatin in water. Stir in sherbet until melted. Stir in pineapple and oranges. Pour into a 2-qt. serving bowl. Chill until firm.

Nutrition Information

- Calories: 77 calories
- Total Fat: 1g
- Cholesterol: 2mg
- Sodium: 17mg
- Total Carbohydrate: 18g
- Protein: 1g
- Fiber: 0 g

105. Fruity Strawberry Gelatin Salad

For a refreshing addition to a potluck or other gathering, Pat Whitten of St. Albans, West Virginia jazzes up gelatin with crushed pineapple, bananas and strawberries. "This salad can be made quickly and is a favorite of my friends," she notes.

Serving: 9 servings. | Prep: 10 m | Cook: 0 m | Ready in: 10 m

Ingredients

- 1 package (6 ounces) strawberry gelatin
- 1 cup boiling water
- 2 packages (12 ounces each) frozen unsweetened strawberries, thawed
- 2 cans (8 ounces each) unsweetened crushed pineapple, undrained
- 3 medium firm bananas, mashed

Direction

- In a bowl, dissolve gelatin in boiling water. Stir in strawberries, pineapple and bananas; mix well. Transfer to a 2-qt. serving bowl. Refrigerate until firm.

Nutrition Information

- Calories: 82 calories
- Total Fat: 0 g
- Cholesterol: 0 mg
- Sodium: 55mg
- Total Carbohydrate: 19g
- Protein: 2g
- Fiber: 3g

106. Gelatin Christmas Ornaments

Muffin tins are the key to making these individual gelatin salads. Once chilled, they're easy to embellish with mayonnaise, sour cream or whipped cream. Maraschino cherries with stems give the look of wire hangers.

Serving: 1 dozen. | Prep: 20 m | Cook: 0 m | Ready in: 20 m

Ingredients

- 3-1/4 cups white grape juice
- 1 package (6 ounces) lime gelatin
- 1 package (6 ounces) raspberry gelatin
- 6 each red and green maraschino cherries with stems
- Mayonnaise, sour cream or whipped cream in a can

Direction

- In a saucepan, bring grape juice to a boil. Place lime gelatin in a bowl; add half of the juice and stir until completely dissolved. Repeat with raspberry gelatin. Pour lime gelatin into six muffin cups (about 1/3 cup in each) coated with cooking spray. Repeat, filling six more cups with raspberry gelatin. Refrigerate for 4 hours or until firm.
- Loosen gelatin around the edges with a sharp knife; invert muffin tin onto waxed paper. Use a metal spatula to transfer to serving plates. Fill a small plastic bag with mayonnaise; cut a small hole in corner of bag. Pipe a small circle near one edge of each ornament; place cherry in center. Decorate ornaments with additional mayonnaise if desired.

Nutrition Information

- Calories: 153 calories
- Total Fat: 0 g
- Cholesterol: 0 mg
- Sodium: 68mg
- Total Carbohydrate: 37g
- Protein: 3g
- Fiber: 0 g

107. Gelatin Fruit Salad

"This gorgeous salad is so refreshing and bursting with flavor that you won't think of it as sugar-free," says Eleanor Mielke of Snohomish, Washington. "A diabetic friend shared the recipe."

Serving: 8 servings. | Prep: 15 m | Cook: 0 m | Ready in: 15 m

Ingredients

- 1 cup unsweetened applesauce
- 1 package (.6 ounces) sugar-free cherry gelatin
- 1 can (12 ounces) or 1-1/2 cups diet ginger ale
- 1 can (8 ounces) unsweetened crushed pineapple, undrained
- Apple slices and fresh mint, optional

Direction

- In a saucepan, bring the applesauce to a boil; remove from the heat.
- Stir in gelatin until dissolved. Slowly add ginger ale and pineapple. Pour into a 2-qt. serving bowl. Chill until set. Garnish with apples and mint if desired.

Nutrition Information

- Calories: 39 calories
- Total Fat: 0 g
- Cholesterol: 0 mg
- Sodium: 66mg
- Total Carbohydrate: 8g
- Protein: 1g
- Fiber: 1g

108. Gelatin Ring with Cream Cheese Balls

Here's a fun way to serve cranberry sauce that will please both kids and adults. The red gelatin and cranberry sauce ring is dressed up with cream cheese balls rolled in ground walnuts. It's cool, colorful and yummy, too! -Jacinta Ransom, South Haven, Michigan

Serving: 10-12 servings. | Prep: 15 m | Cook: 0 m | Ready in: 15 m

Ingredients

- 2 packages (3 ounces each) raspberry gelatin
- 2 cups boiling water
- 2 cans (16 ounces each) whole-berry cranberry sauce
- 1 package (8 ounces) cream cheese
- 1 cup ground walnuts

Direction

- In a large bowl, dissolve gelatin in boiling water. Stir in cranberry sauce until well blended. Pour into a 6-cup ring mold coated with cooking spray; refrigerate overnight or until firm.
- Roll cream cheese into 3/4-in. balls; coat with walnuts. Unmold gelatin onto a serving platter; place the cream cheese balls in the center of the ring.

Nutrition Information

- Calories: 189 calories
- Total Fat: 11g
- Cholesterol: 21mg
- Sodium: 80mg
- Total Carbohydrate: 22g
- Protein: 3g
- Fiber: 1g

109. Gingered Lime Gelatin

This recipe calls for ginger ale in place of cold water, which gives the salad a "tingly" taste and heightens the ginger flavor.--Sandra McKenzie, Braham, Minnesota

Serving: 12 servings. | Prep: 10 m | Cook: 0 m | Ready in: 10 m

Ingredients

- 1 can (20 ounces) pineapple tidbits
- 1 package (6 ounces) lime gelatin
- 1-1/2 cups boiling water
- 1 cup ginger ale, chilled
- 1/4 teaspoon ground ginger

Direction

- Drain pineapple, reserving juice; set the pineapple aside. In a bowl, dissolve the gelatin in water. Stir in ginger ale, ginger and the reserved juice. Chill until syrupy, about 45 minutes. Fold in pineapple. Transfer to a 6-cup mold coated with cooking spray. Refrigerate until firm. Unmold onto a serving platter.

Nutrition Information

- Calories: 21 calories
- Total Fat: 1g
- Cholesterol: 0 mg
- Sodium: 37mg
- Total Carbohydrate: 4g
- Protein: 1g
- Fiber: 0 g

110. Golden Glow Gelatin Mold

I make this Jello mold recipe for many a party and not one bite is ever left. – Aline Savoie, Edmonton, Alberta

Serving: 12-16 servings. | Prep: 15 m | Cook: 0 m | Ready in: 15 m

Ingredients

- 2 cans (8 ounces each) crushed pineapple
- 30 large marshmallows
- 1 package (6 ounces) lemon gelatin
- 2 cups boiling water
- 3 ounces cream cheese, softened
- 1 cup cold water
- 1-1/2 cups shredded carrots
- Leaf lettuce and lemon slices, optional

Direction

- Drain pineapple, reserving juice; set the pineapple aside. In a large saucepan, combine pineapple juice and marshmallows; cook and stir over low heat until marshmallows are melted. Remove from the heat.
- Dissolve gelatin in boiling water. Add cream cheese; stir until mixture is thoroughly blended. Stir in cold water and marshmallow mixture. Chill until partially set. Fold in carrots and pineapple.
- Pour into a 6-cup mold coated with cooking spray. Refrigerate until set. Unmold onto a lettuce-lined serving plate if desired. Garnish with lemon slices if desired.

Nutrition Information

- Calories: 113 calories
- Total Fat: 2g
- Cholesterol: 6mg
- Sodium: 50mg
- Total Carbohydrate: 24g
- Protein: 2g
- Fiber: 0 g

111. Golden Glow Salad

"MY SISTER and I loved this salad because we thought it tasted like a dessert. We ate a lot of Jell-O when we were growing up, but this was our favorite gelatin dish. I always make this salad for picnics. I provides a fruit and a vegetable, and bright color as well."

Serving: 6 servings. | Prep: 15 m | Cook: 0 m | Ready in: 15 m

Ingredients

- 1 package (3 ounces) orange gelatin
- 1 cup boiling water
- 1 can (8 ounces) crushed pineapple
- 1 tablespoon lemon juice
- Cold water
- 1/4 teaspoon salt, optional
- 3/4 cup finely shredded carrots

Direction

- In a bowl, dissolve gelatin in boiling water. Drain pineapple, reserving juice. Add lemon juice and enough cold water to pineapple juice to make 1 cup; add salt if desired. Stir into gelatin. Chill until slightly set. Stir in pineapple and carrots. Pour into an oiled 4-cup mold; cover and chill until firm. Unmold.

Nutrition Information

- Calories: 35 calories
- Total Fat: 0 g
- Cholesterol: 0 mg
- Sodium: 42mg
- Total Carbohydrate: 8g
- Protein: 1g
- Fiber: 0 g

112.Grandmas Gelatin Fruit Salad

Whenever I invite my big family for dinner, my grandchildren request this favorite fruit salad. My sons have always liked it, too - maybe the taste runs in our family! This salad is also good for potluck gatherings.

Serving: 12-15 servings. | Prep: 20 m | Cook: 5 m | Ready in: 25 m

Ingredients

- 2 cups boiling water, divided
- 1 package (3 ounces) lemon gelatin
- 2 cups ice cubes, divided
- 1 can (20 ounces) crushed pineapple, liquid drained and reserved
- 1 package (3 ounces) orange gelatin
- 2 cups miniature marshmallows
- 1/2 cup sugar
- 2 tablespoons cornstarch
- 1 cup reserved pineapple juice
- 1 large egg, lightly beaten
- 1 tablespoon butter
- 3 large bananas, sliced
- 1 cup whipped topping
- 1/2 cup finely shredded cheddar cheese

Direction

- In a large bowl, combine 1 cup water and lemon gelatin. Add 1 cup ice cubes, stirring until melted. Stir in pineapple. Pour into a 13x9-in. dish coated with cooking spray; refrigerate until set but not firm.
- Repeat with the orange gelatin, remaining water and ice. Stir in marshmallows. Pour over lemon layer; refrigerate until firm.
- Meanwhile, in a small saucepan, combine sugar and cornstarch. Stir in reserved pineapple juice until smooth. Cook and stir over medium-high heat until thickened and bubbly. Reduce heat; cook and stir 2 minutes longer. Remove from the heat.
- Stir a small amount of hot filling into egg; return all to the pan, stirring constantly. Bring to a gentle boil; cook and stir 2 minutes longer. Remove from the heat; stir in butter. Cool to

room temperature without stirring. Refrigerate for 1 hour or until chilled.

- Arrange bananas over gelatin. Stir whipped topping into dressing. Spread over bananas. Sprinkle with cheese.

Nutrition Information

- Calories: 194 calories
- Total Fat: 3g
- Cholesterol: 20mg
- Sodium: 64mg
- Total Carbohydrate: 40g
- Protein: 3g
- Fiber: 1g

113. Grandmothers Orange Salad

This gelatin salad is slightly sweet and tangy, too. It adds beautiful color to any meal and appeals to appetites of all ages! --Ann Eastman, Greenville, California

Serving: 10 servings. | Prep: 20 m | Cook: 0 m | Ready in: 20 m

Ingredients

- 1 can (11 ounces) mandarin oranges
- 1 can (8 ounces) crushed pineapple
- Water
- 1 package (6 ounces) orange gelatin
- 1 pint orange sherbet, softened
- 2 bananas, sliced

Direction

- Drain oranges and pineapple, reserving juices. Set oranges and pineapple aside. Add water to juices to measure 2 cups. Place in a saucepan and bring to a boil; pour over gelatin in a large bowl. Stir until gelatin is dissolved. Stir in sherbet until smooth.
- Chill until partially set (watch carefully). Fold in oranges, pineapple and bananas. Pour into an oiled 6-cup mold. Chill until firm.

Nutrition Information

- Calories: 161 calories
- Total Fat: 1g
- Cholesterol: 2mg
- Sodium: 55mg
- Total Carbohydrate: 39g
- Protein: 2g
- Fiber: 1g

114. Grapefruit Gelatin

We have no idea where this recipe originated, but this unique salad is always well received. It's a popular choice with a sandwich for our luncheon combinations and is also served as a dinner side dish. Many people prefer it to a tossed salad.--Watts Bar Resort, Joyce Probst, Watts Bar Dam, Tennessee

Serving: 30 servings. | Prep: 20 m | Cook: 0 m | Ready in: 20 m

Ingredients

- 8 jars (16 ounces each) grapefruit sections
- 1 cup water
- 8 envelopes unflavored gelatin
- 2 cups sugar
- 2 to 3 teaspoons salt
- 1/3 cup lemon juice

Direction

- Drain grapefruit, reserving 6 cups juice; set fruit and 4 cups of juice aside. In a saucepan, combine 2 cups juice, water and gelatin; let stand for 1 minute. Cook and stir over low heat until gelatin is dissolved. Remove from the heat. Add sugar and salt; stir until dissolved. Add lemon juice and reserved grapefruit and juice. Pour into two 13-in. x 9-in. pans. Cover and refrigerate until set.

Nutrition Information

- Calories: 63 calories
- Total Fat: 0 g

- Cholesterol: 0 mg
- Sodium: 161mg
- Total Carbohydrate: 15g
- Protein: 2g
- Fiber: 0 g

115. Grapefruit Gelatin Molds

I found this recipe in a magazine back in the '50s. It's a nice salad, particularly with a heavy meal. It's a refreshing snack as well.

Serving: 2-3 servings. | Prep: 10 m | Cook: 10 m | Ready in: 20 m

Ingredients

- 1 envelope unflavored gelatin
- 2 tablespoons cold water
- 1/3 cup sugar
- 1/3 cup water
- 1/2 cup grapefruit juice
- 3 tablespoons orange juice
- 4 teaspoons lemon juice

Direction

- In a small bowl, sprinkle gelatin over cold water; let stand for 1 minute. In a saucepan, combine sugar and water; bring to a boil. Reduce heat; stir in gelatin until dissolved. Stir in juices; pour into three 1/2-cup or one 2-cup mold coated with cooking spray. Refrigerate for 4-5 hours or until set.

Nutrition Information

- Calories: 118 calories
- Total Fat: 0 g
- Cholesterol: 0 mg
- Sodium: 5mg
- Total Carbohydrate: 28g
- Protein: 2g
- Fiber: 0 g

116. Green Flop Jello

Get ready for fluffy lemon-lime goodness. Try it with any flavor Jell-O! --Michelle Gauer, Spicer, Minnesota

Serving: 16 servings (3/4 cup each). | Prep: 15 m | Cook: 0 m | Ready in: 15 m

Ingredients

- 2 cups lemon-lime soda
- 2 packages (3 ounces each) lime gelatin
- 6 ounces cream cheese, softened
- 2 cups lemon-lime soda, chilled
- 1 carton (12 ounces) frozen whipped topping, thawed

Direction

- Microwave 2 cups soda on high for 1-2 minutes or until hot. Place hot soda and gelatin in a blender; cover and process until gelatin is dissolved. Add cream cheese; process until blended.
- Transfer to a large bowl; stir in chilled soda. Whisk in whipped topping. Pour into a 3-qt. trifle bowl or glass bowl. Refrigerate, covered, 4 hours or until firm.

Nutrition Information

- Calories: 159 calories
- Total Fat: 7g
- Cholesterol: 12mg
- Sodium: 62mg
- Total Carbohydrate: 21g
- Protein: 2g
- Fiber: 0 g

117. Hidden Pear Salad

Light and fluffy, this colorful salad is a very flavorful family favorite. When I made it for my husband's family before we were married, we all joked about not being able to find any pears, so the name stuck.

Serving: 6-8 servings. | Prep: 15 m | Cook: 0 m | Ready in: 15 m

Ingredients

- 1 can (16 ounces) pears, liquid drained and reserved
- 1 package (3 ounces) lime gelatin
- 3 ounces cream cheese, softened
- 1/4 teaspoon lemon juice
- 1 envelope whipped topping mix (Dream Whip)
- Lettuce leaves

Direction

- In a saucepan, bring pear liquid to a boil. Stir in gelatin until dissolved. Remove from the heat; cool at room temperature until syrupy. Meanwhile, puree pears in a blender.
- In a bowl, beat cream cheese and lemon juice until fluffy and smooth. Add pureed pears and mix well. Prepare whipped topping according to package directions; fold into pear mixture. Fold in cooled gelatin.
- Pour into a 4-1/2-cup mold that has been coated with cooking spray. Chill overnight. Just before serving, unmold salad onto a lettuce-lined platter.

Nutrition Information

- Calories: 139 calories
- Total Fat: 5g
- Cholesterol: 12mg
- Sodium: 60mg
- Total Carbohydrate: 22g
- Protein: 2g
- Fiber: 0 g

118. Holiday Cranberry Gelatin Salad

This light, delicious holiday salad is very popular in my family and has been requested every year since I first brought it to Christmas Eve dinner. The refreshing, not-too-sweet flavor is a perfect pairing with just about any meat. —Jennifer Mastnick, Hartville, Ohio

Serving: 12 servings. | Prep: 30 m | Cook: 0 m | Ready in: 30 m

Ingredients

- 2 packages (3 ounces each) raspberry gelatin
- 2 cups boiling water, divided
- 1 can (14 ounces) whole-berry cranberry sauce
- 2 tablespoons lemon juice
- 1 cup heavy whipping cream
- 1 package (8 ounces) cream cheese, softened
- 1/2 cup chopped pecans

Direction

- In a small bowl, dissolve gelatin in 1 cup boiling water. In another bowl, combine cranberry sauce and remaining water; add gelatin mixture and lemon juice. Pour into a 13-in. x 9-in. dish coated with cooking spray; refrigerate until firm, about 1 hour.
- In a large bowl, beat cream until stiff peaks form. In another bowl, beat cream cheese until smooth. Stir in 1/2 cup whipped cream; fold in remaining whipped cream. Spread over gelatin mixture; sprinkle with pecans. Refrigerate for at least 2 hours.

Nutrition Information

- Calories: 241 calories
- Total Fat: 14g
- Cholesterol: 34mg
- Sodium: 100mg
- Total Carbohydrate: 28g
- Protein: 3g
- Fiber: 1g

119. Holiday Cranberry Salad

My mom made this every Thanksgiving and Christmas, and I have continued the tradition. We now are on our fourth generation of sharing and enjoying this salad, as my grandson makes a special request for it every year. I also serve this as a side dish when I make a chicken pot pie. -- Peggy Tagge, Stokesdale, North Carolina

Serving: 12 servings (1/2 cup each). | Prep: 10 m | Cook: 0 m | Ready in: 10 m

Ingredients

- 1-1/2 cups boiling water
- 1 package (3 ounces) lemon gelatin
- 1 package (3 ounces) cherry gelatin
- 1 can (14 ounces) whole-berry cranberry sauce
- 1 can (20 ounces) crushed pineapple, undrained
- 1 celery rib, finely chopped
- 1/2 cup chopped pecans

Direction

- In a large bowl, add boiling water to gelatins; stir 2 minutes to completely dissolve. Stir in cranberry sauce. Refrigerate 30-40 minutes or until slightly thickened. Stir in pineapple, celery and pecans. Transfer to a 6-cup ring mold coated with cooking spray. Refrigerate 4 hours or until set.

Nutrition Information

- Calories:
- Total Fat: g
- Cholesterol: mg
- Sodium: mg
- Total Carbohydrate: g
- Protein: g
- Fiber: g

120. Holiday Gelatin Mold

No matter where I take this attractive salad, I'm asked to share the recipe. With its red and green layers, it dresses up any holiday buffet. I'm a retired teacher who loves to cook-especially dishes I can make ahead, like this one.

Serving: 16 servings. | Prep: 02 h 00 m | Cook: 0 m | Ready in: 02 h 00 m

Ingredients

- 1 can (8 ounces) sliced pineapple
- 1 package (3 ounces) lime gelatin
- 4 cups boiling water, divided
- 2 tablespoons lemon juice
- 1 package (3 ounces) lemon gelatin
- 6 ounces cream cheese, softened
- 1/3 cup mayonnaise
- 1 package (3 ounces) raspberry gelatin
- 2 medium firm bananas

Direction

- Drain pineapple, reserving juice. In a bowl, dissolve lime gelatin in 1 cup boiling water. Combine the pineapple juice, lemon juice and enough cold water to measure 1 cup; add to dissolved gelatin. Cut pineapple slices in half; arrange on the bottom of a 12-cup ring mold coated with cooking spray.
- Pour a small amount of lime gelatin over the pineapple; refrigerate until set. Add remaining lime gelatin; refrigerate until firm. In a small bowl, dissolve lemon gelatin in 1 cup boiling water. Refrigerate until partially set. Beat until light and fluffy.
- In another small bowl, beat cream cheese until fluffy. Stir in the mayonnaise. Fold in whipped gelatin; pour over lime layer. Refrigerate until firm.
- Dissolve raspberry gelatin in remaining boiling water. Slice bananas; place over lemon layer. Carefully spoon the raspberry gelatin over bananas. Refrigerate until firm or overnight.

Nutrition Information

- Calories: 131 calories

- Total Fat: 6g
- Cholesterol: 8mg
- Sodium: 78mg
- Total Carbohydrate: 19g
- Protein: 2g
- Fiber: 0 g

- Calories: 105 calories
- Total Fat: 1g
- Cholesterol: 1mg
- Sodium: 62mg
- Total Carbohydrate: 24g
- Protein: 1g
- Fiber: 1g

121.Holiday Gelatin Salad

Because I care for a teenager with diabetes, I decided to change my annual holiday salad so she could have some. -- Mareen Robinson, Spanish Fork, Utah

Serving: 12 servings (3/4 cup topping). | Prep: 25 m | Cook: 0 m | Ready in: 25 m

Ingredients

- 1 package (.3 ounce) sugar-free lemon gelatin
- 1 package (.3 ounce) sugar-free strawberry gelatin
- 1 package (.3 ounce) sugar-free cherry gelatin
- 1-3/4 cups boiling water
- 1 can (20 ounces) unsweetened crushed pineapple
- 1 can (14 ounces) whole-berry cranberry sauce
- 1 medium navel orange, peeled and sectioned
- 3/4 cup reduced-fat whipped topping
- 1/4 cup fat-free sour cream

Direction

- In a large bowl, dissolve the gelatins in boiling water. Drain pineapple, reserving juice in a 2-cup measuring cup; add enough cold water to measure 2 cups. Stir into gelatin mixture.
- Place the pineapple, cranberry sauce and orange in a food processor; cover and pulse until blended. Stir into gelatin mixture. Transfer to an 8-cup ring mold coated with cooking spray. Refrigerate until firm.
- In a small bowl, combine whipped topping and sour cream. Unmold gelatin; serve with topping.

122. Holiday Ribbon Gelatin

Layers of red and green make this festive salad a favorite during the Christmas season. Kids are sure to find it fun to eat, and adults will enjoy the combination of sweet-tart flavors. —Jenny Hughson, Mitchell, Nebraska

Serving: 12-15 servings. | Prep: 40 m | Cook: 0 m | Ready in: 40 m

Ingredients

- 2 packages (3 ounces each) lime gelatin
- 5 cups boiling water, divided
- 4 cups cold water, divided
- 1 package (3 ounces) lemon gelatin
- 1/2 cup miniature marshmallows
- 1 package (8 ounces) cream cheese, softened
- 1 cup mayonnaise
- 1 can (8 ounces) crushed pineapple, undrained
- 2 packages (3 ounces each) cherry gelatin

Direction

- In a large bowl, dissolve lime gelatin in 2 cups boiling water. Add 2 cups cold water; stir. Pour into a 13-in. x 9-in. dish; refrigerate until firm but not set, about 1 hour.
- In a large bowl, dissolve lemon gelatin in 1 cup boiling water. Stir in marshmallows until melted. Cool for 20 minutes. In a small bowl, beat cream cheese and mayonnaise until smooth. Gradually beat in lemon gelatin. Stir in pineapple. Carefully spoon over the lime layer. Chill until firm but not set.
- Dissolve cherry gelatin in 2 cups boiling water. Add remaining cold water; stir. Spoon over

the lemon layer. Refrigerate entire gelatin salad overnight. Cut into squares to serve.

Nutrition Information

- Calories: 236 calories
- Total Fat: 17g
- Cholesterol: 22mg
- Sodium: 164mg
- Total Carbohydrate: 19g
- Protein: 3g
- Fiber: 0 g

123. Igloo Salad

Miniature marshmallows cover this fluffy fruit salad that's fashioned into an Eskimo igloo. The cool mixture inside is a breeze to make with canned fruit and whipped topping.

Serving: 6 servings. | Prep: 30 m | Cook: 0 m | Ready in: 30 m

Ingredients

- 1 can (15-1/4 ounces) fruit cocktail, drained
- 1 can (11 ounces) mandarin oranges, drained
- 1/2 cup sweetened shredded coconut
- 1-3/4 cups whipped topping, divided
- 2-1/2 cups miniature marshmallows, divided

Direction

- In a bowl, combine the fruit cocktail, oranges, coconut, 1 cup whipped topping and 1/2 cup marshmallows. Spoon into two balls, one 5-1/2 in. and one 3-1/2 in.
- On a serving plate, with smaller ball in front of larger ball. Spoon out some salad from small ball to make a doorway. Cover with remaining whipped topping and marshmallows.

Nutrition Information

- Calories: 248 calories
- Total Fat: 6g
- Cholesterol: 0 mg
- Sodium: 38mg

- Total Carbohydrate: 47g
- Protein: 1g
- Fiber: 1g

124. Jazzy Gelatin

Finish things off with a bang with this colorful gelatin garnished with a chorus of fresh grapes. Chock-full of mandarin oranges and crushed pineapple, it's so refreshing that guests won't be able to refrain from seconds. --Taste of Home Test Kitchen, Milwaukee, Wisconsin

Serving: 12 servings. | Prep: 10 m | Cook: 0 m | Ready in: 10 m

Ingredients

- 1 package (6 ounces) orange gelatin
- 2 cups boiling water
- 1 cup ice cubes
- 1 can (15 ounces) mandarin oranges, drained
- 1 can (8 ounces) unsweetened crushed pineapple, undrained
- 1 can (6 ounces) frozen orange juice concentrate, thawed
- Green grapes and fresh mint, optional

Direction

- In a large bowl, dissolve gelatin in boiling water. Add ice cubes, oranges, pineapple and orange juice concentrate. Pour into a 6-cup ring mold coated with cooking spray. Refrigerate overnight or until firm.
- Just before serving, unmold onto a serving plate. Fill center with grapes and garnish with mint if desired.

Nutrition Information

- Calories: 107 calories
- Total Fat: 0 g
- Cholesterol: 0 mg
- Sodium: 35mg
- Total Carbohydrate: 26g
- Protein: 2g
- Fiber: 1g

125. Jiggly Applesauce

My cousin Dave brings this to our annual family cookout. If you can't find Red Hots, grab a jar of cinnamon applesauce instead. --Josh Hoppert, Cudahy, Wisconsin

Serving: 8 servings. | Prep: 10 m | Cook: 0 m | Ready in: 10 m

Ingredients

- 2 cups boiling water
- 1/4 cup Red Hots, crushed
- 2 packages (3 ounces each) strawberry gelatin
- 2 cups cold unsweetened applesauce
- Finely chopped fresh strawberries, optional

Direction

- Add boiling water and crushed Red Hots to gelatin. Stir 2 minutes to completely dissolve gelatin and candy. Stir in cold applesauce. Pour into individual serving glasses or an 8-in. square dish. Refrigerate until firm, about 2 hours. If desired, serve with finely chopped strawberries.

Nutrition Information

- Calories: 130 calories
- Total Fat: 0 g
- Cholesterol: 0 mg
- Sodium: 50mg
- Total Carbohydrate: 32g
- Protein: 2g
- Fiber: 1g

126. Layered Berry Gelatin Salad

"This bright, citrusy salad is a combination of several recipes," writes Sharen Clark from Sunnyside, Washington. "I love to serve it with Thanksgiving and Christmas meals."

Serving: 15 servings. | Prep: 20 m | Cook: 5 m | Ready in: 25 m

Ingredients

- 1 package (.3 ounce) sugar-free raspberry gelatin
- 1 cup boiling water
- 1 can (14 ounces) jellied cranberry sauce
- CREAM LAYER:
- 1 envelope unflavored gelatin
- 1/2 cup cold water
- 2 cups (16 ounces) reduced-fat sour cream
- 1 teaspoon vanilla extract
- 1 cup reduced-fat whipped topping
- ORANGE LAYER:
- 2 cans (11 ounces each) mandarin oranges
- 1 package (.3 ounce) sugar-free orange gelatin
- 1 cup boiling water

Direction

- In a small bowl, dissolve raspberry gelatin in boiling water. Whisk in cranberry sauce until blended. Transfer to a 13-in. x 9-in. dish coated with cooking spray. Refrigerate until set but not firm, about 45 minutes.
- For the cream layer, in a small saucepan, sprinkle gelatin over cold water. Let stand for 1 minute. Heat over low heat, stirring until gelatin is completely dissolved. Cool to room temperature.
- In a small bowl, combine sour cream and vanilla. Fold in gelatin mixture, then whipped topping. Spoon over cranberry layer and gently spread. Refrigerate until set but not firm, about 45 minutes.
- Drain oranges, reserving 1 cup syrup; set oranges aside. In a small bowl, dissolve orange gelatin in boiling water. Sir in reserved syrup. Refrigerate until slightly thickened, about 45 minutes. Stir in oranges. Carefully spoon over

sour cream layer. Cover and refrigerate for 8 hours or overnight.

Nutrition Information

- Calories: 129 calories
- Total Fat: 3g
- Cholesterol: 11mg
- Sodium: 58mg
- Total Carbohydrate: 21g
- Protein: 3g
- Fiber: 1g

127. Layered Christmas Gelatin

Christmastime always means that this recipe comes out of my recipe box. The traditional holiday colors in this salad make the buffet table look so pretty. --Diane Schefelker, Ireton, Iowa

Serving: 10 servings. | Prep: 30 m | Cook: 0 m | Ready in: 30 m

Ingredients

- 1 package (3 ounces) lime gelatin
- 1 cup boiling water
- 1/3 cup unsweetened pineapple juice
- 1 cup crushed pineapple, drained
- CREAM CHEESE LAYER:
- 1 teaspoon unflavored gelatin
- 2 tablespoons cold water
- 1 package (8 ounces) cream cheese, softened
- 1/3 cup milk
- BERRY LAYER:
- 2 packages (3 ounces each) strawberry gelatin
- 2 cups boiling water
- 1 can (14 ounces) whole-berry cranberry sauce
- Optional ingredients: thawed whipped topping, lime wedges and fresh strawberries

Direction

- Dissolve lime gelatin in boiling water; stir in pineapple juice. Stir in pineapple. Pour into an 11x7-in. dish; refrigerate until set.
- In a small saucepan, sprinkle unflavored gelatin over cold water; let stand for 1 minute.

Heat over low heat, stirring until gelatin is completely dissolved. Transfer to a small bowl. Beat in cream cheese and milk until smooth. Spread over lime layer; refrigerate until set.
- Dissolve strawberry gelatin in boiling water; stir in cranberry sauce. Cool for 10 minutes. Carefully spoon over cream cheese layer. Refrigerate until set.
- Cut into squares. Serve, if desired, with whipped topping, lime wedges and fresh strawberries.

Nutrition Information

- Calories: 267 calories
- Total Fat: 8g
- Cholesterol: 26mg
- Sodium: 139mg
- Total Carbohydrate: 46g
- Protein: 5g
- Fiber: 1g

128. Layered Cranberry Gelatin Salad

Light and tangy, this gelatin is guaranteed to please. Kids go crazy for the marshmallow-cream cheese layer on top. – Irma Senner, Dixmont, Maine

Serving: 12 servings. | Prep: 20 m | Cook: 0 m | Ready in: 20 m

Ingredients

- CRANBERRY LAYER:
- 1 package (3 ounces) cranberry or raspberry gelatin
- 1 cup boiling water
- 1 can (14 ounces) whole-berry cranberry sauce
- LEMON LAYER:
- 1 package (3 ounces) lemon gelatin
- 1 cup boiling water
- 3 ounces cream cheese, softened
- 1/3 cup mayonnaise
- 1 can (8 ounces) crushed pineapple, undrained

- 1/2 cup heavy whipping cream, whipped
- 1 cup miniature marshmallows
- 2 tablespoons chopped pecans

Direction

- In a small bowl, dissolve cranberry gelatin in boiling water; stir in cranberry sauce until blended. Transfer to an 8-in. square dish. Refrigerate until set.
- In another bowl, dissolve lemon gelatin in boiling water. Beat cream cheese and mayonnaise until smooth; stir into the lemon gelatin with the pineapple. Refrigerate until slightly thickened, about 2 hours.
- Fold the cream, marshmallows and pecans into cream cheese mixture. Spread over cranberry layer. Refrigerate for 4 hours or until set.

Nutrition Information

- Calories: 239 calories
- Total Fat: 12g
- Cholesterol: 24mg
- Sodium: 100mg
- Total Carbohydrate: 32g
- Protein: 2g
- Fiber: 1g

129. Layered Gelatin Salad

It's nice to offer a cool gelatin salad as an alternate to hot side dishes. Make it ahead and relax a little on the day of your party.

Serving: 8-10 servings. | Prep: 15 m | Cook: 10 m | Ready in: 25 m

Ingredients

- 1 package (3 ounces) lemon gelatin
- 2-1/2 cups boiling water, divided
- 2 cans (8 ounces each) crushed pineapple
- 1 package (8 ounces) cream cheese, softened
- 1/4 cup mayonnaise
- 1/4 cup whipped topping

- 1 envelope unflavored gelatin
- 3/4 cup cold water, divided
- 1 package (3 ounces) lime gelatin

Direction

- In a bowl, dissolve lemon gelatin in 1-1/2 cups boiling water. Drain pineapple, reserving 2/3 cup juice; set juice aside. Stir pineapple into gelatin. Pour into a 2-qt. glass bowl. Cover and refrigerate until firm.
- In a small bowl, combine cream cheese, mayonnaise and whipped topping; set aside. Sprinkle unflavored gelatin over 1/4 cup cold water; let stand for 1 minute. In a small saucepan, bring the reserved pineapple juice to a boil; stir in dissolved unflavored gelatin. Add to the cream cheese mixture; mix well. Carefully spread over the chilled lemon layer. Refrigerate until firm.
- In a bowl, dissolve lime gelatin in remaining boiling water. Stir in remaining cold water. Chill until partially set. Beat with a portable mixer until foamy. Pour over cream cheese layer. Refrigerate until firm, about 3 hours or overnight.

Nutrition Information

- Calories: 206 calories
- Total Fat: 13g
- Cholesterol: 27mg
- Sodium: 137mg
- Total Carbohydrate: 20g
- Protein: 4g
- Fiber: 0 g

130. Layered Orange Gelatin

"I reduced the calories and fat in a tangy gelatin recipe my mom gave me," explains Angie Philkill of Zeeland, Michigan. The lovely molded salad forms layers as it chills. "We especially enjoy it with ham," she adds.

Serving: 10 servings. | Prep: 15 m | Cook: 0 m | Ready in: 15 m

Ingredients

- 2 packages (.3 ounce each) sugar-free orange gelatin
- 2 cups boiling water
- 1 can (15 ounces) mandarin oranges
- 3 ounces reduced-fat cream cheese, cubed
- 1 pint orange sherbet, softened
- 1-1/2 cups reduced-fat whipped topping

Direction

- In a bowl, dissolve gelatin in boiling water. Drain oranges, reserving the juice; set oranges aside. Stir juice into gelatin. Add cream cheese; beat until smooth. Stir in sherbet and whipped topping. Pour into a 6-cup ring mold coated with cooking spray. Top with oranges. Cover and refrigerate overnight.

Nutrition Information

- Calories: 125 calories
- Total Fat: 4g
- Cholesterol: 20mg
- Sodium: 90mg
- Total Carbohydrate: 20g
- Protein: 2g
- Fiber: 0 g

131. Lime Chiffon Jello

As kids, we always looked forward to my aunt bringing this wonderful dish to Thanksgiving and Christmas dinner. -- Mary Richart, Roaring Branch, Pennsylvania

Serving: 12 servings. | Prep: 25 m | Cook: 0 m | Ready in: 25 m

Ingredients

- 1 package (3 ounces) lime gelatin
- 1/4 cup sugar
- 1 cup boiling water
- 1 can (12 ounces) evaporated milk
- 3/4 cup graham cracker crumbs
- 3 tablespoons butter, melted

Direction

- Place gelatin and sugar in a bowl. Add boiling water to gelatin mixture; stir 2 minutes to completely dissolve. Refrigerate until very thick, about 30 minutes.
- Meanwhile, place milk and mixer beaters in a bowl. Freeze until ice crystals form around edge of bowl, about 30 minutes. Beat milk on high speed until light and fluffy. While beating, pour in thickened jello mixture; beat on high until soft peaks form.
- Pour into an 11x7-in. dish. Mix cracker crumbs and butter; sprinkle over top. Refrigerate, covered, at least 4 hours before serving.

Nutrition Information

- Calories:
- Total Fat: g
- Cholesterol: mg
- Sodium: mg
- Total Carbohydrate: g
- Protein: g
- Fiber: g

132. Lime Delight

CREATED by my husband's cousin, this salad appeared in her church's recipe book. Since it's quick and easy to prepare, I make it often for my husband and me now that we're "empty nesters". It's light and attractive. -Nancy Vavrinek, Adrian, Michigan

Serving: 2 servings. | Prep: 10 m | Cook: 0 m | Ready in: 10 m

Ingredients

- 1 can (8 ounces) crushed pineapple, undrained
- 1/4 cup lime gelatin powder
- 1/2 cup cream-style cottage cheese
- 1 cup whipped topping

Direction

- In a small saucepan, bring pineapple to a boil over medium heat. Remove from the heat; stir in gelatin until dissolved. Chill until slightly thickened, about 30 minutes. Stir in cottage cheese and whipped topping. Cover and refrigerate until thickened.

Nutrition Information

- Calories: 329 calories
- Total Fat: 9g
- Cholesterol: 8mg
- Sodium: 293mg
- Total Carbohydrate: 52g
- Protein: 10g
- Fiber: 1g

133. Lime Gelatin Salad

I've made this refreshing recipe more than 100 times over the past 15 years! It can be a salad or dessert. When I take it to a potluck, it's always one of the first things to disappear. -Louise Harding, Newburgh, New York

Serving: 16-20 servings. | Prep: 15 m | Cook: 0 m | Ready in: 15 m

Ingredients

- 1 package (6 ounces) lime gelatin
- 1 cup boiling water
- 1 package (8 ounces) cream cheese, softened
- 1/2 teaspoon vanilla extract
- 1 can (15 ounces) mandarin oranges, drained
- 1 can (8 ounces) crushed pineapple, drained
- 1 cup lemon-lime soda
- 1/2 cup chopped pecans
- 1 carton (8 ounces) frozen whipped topping, thawed, divided

Direction

- Dissolve gelatin in water. In a bowl, beat cream cheese until fluffy. Stir in gelatin mixture and beat until smooth. Stir in vanilla, oranges, pineapple, soda and pecans. Chill until the mixture mounds slightly when dropped from a spoon. Fold in three-fourths of the whipped topping. Pour into a 13x9-in. dish. Refrigerate for 3-4 hours or until firm. Cut into squares; garnish with the remaining whipped topping.

Nutrition Information

- Calories: 147 calories
- Total Fat: 8g
- Cholesterol: 12mg
- Sodium: 56mg
- Total Carbohydrate: 17g
- Protein: 2g
- Fiber: 1g

134. Lime Pear Salad

Through my years of working in the food service industry, I've collected a bounty of salad recipes. This pleasantly colored side dish is cool, creamy and comforting.

Serving: 6-8 servings. | Prep: 20 m | Cook: 0 m | Ready in: 20 m

Ingredients

- 3 ounces cream cheese, softened
- 1 package (3 ounces) lime gelatin
- 1 can (16 ounces) pear halves
- 2 cups vanilla ice cream, softened

Direction

- In a bowl, beat cream cheese and gelatin until smooth. Drain pears, reserving syrup; set pears aside. If necessary, add enough water to syrup to equals 1 cup.
- In a small saucepan, bring syrup to a boil. Gradually add to gelatin mixture, beating until smooth. Stir in ice cream until dissolved. Mash pears and fold into gelatin mixture. Pour into a greased 6-cup mold. Chill until firm.

Nutrition Information

- Calories: 184 calories
- Total Fat: 7g
- Cholesterol: 26mg
- Sodium: 85mg
- Total Carbohydrate: 28g
- Protein: 3g
- Fiber: 1g

135. Lime Sherbet Molded Salad

For an eye-appealing addition to a picnic, potluck or other gathering, try this molded gelatin salad. With lovely color, creamy texture and refreshing flavor, it's sure to disappear in a jiffy. --Cyndi Fynaardt, Oskaloosa, Iowa

Serving: 16 servings. | Prep: 20 m | Cook: 0 m | Ready in: 20 m

Ingredients

- 2 packages (3 ounces each) lime gelatin
- 2 cups boiling water
- 2 pints lime sherbet, softened
- 1 carton (8 ounces) whipped topping, thawed

Direction

- In a large bowl, dissolve gelatin in boiling water. Stir in sherbet until well blended. Chill until syrupy.
- Spoon whipped topping into a large bowl. Gradually beat in the gelatin mixture on low speed until well blended. Pour into a 12-cup mold coated with cooking spray. Refrigerate for 6-8 hours or until set.

Nutrition Information

- Calories: 110 calories
- Total Fat: 3g
- Cholesterol: 2mg
- Sodium: 29mg
- Total Carbohydrate: 19g
- Protein: 1g
- Fiber: 0 g

136. Lime Strawberry Surprise

Eye-catching in Christmas colors, this dish looks deliciously decorative on the table. Its combination of fruitiness and nutty crunch is surprisingly simple to create. --Arline Wertz, Millington, Tennessee

Serving: 8-10 servings. | Prep: 20 m | Cook: 0 m | Ready in: 20 m

Ingredients

- 1 package (3 ounces) lime gelatin
- 1 can (8 ounces) crushed pineapple, drained
- 1 package (8 ounces) cream cheese, softened
- 1/2 cup mayonnaise
- 1/2 cup chopped pecans
- 1 package (3 ounces) cherry or strawberry gelatin

Direction

- Prepare lime gelatin according to package directions. Refrigerate until partially set, about 1 hour. Stir in pineapple. Pour into an 8-cup bowl or mold coated with cooking spray. Cover and refrigerate until firm, about 3 hours.
- In a small bowl, beat cream cheese and mayonnaise until smooth; stir in pecans. Spread over lime gelatin. Refrigerate until firm, about 2 hours.
- Prepare strawberry gelatin according to package directions; cool slightly. Carefully spoon over cream cheese layer. Refrigerate until firm about 3 hours or overnight.

Nutrition Information

- Calories: 276 calories
- Total Fat: 21g
- Cholesterol: 29mg
- Sodium: 166mg
- Total Carbohydrate: 20g
- Protein: 4g
- Fiber: 1g

137. LimePear Gelatin Bells

For a festive flair, I use bell-shaped molds for this gelatin salad, but use whatever molds you have on hand. It's such a refreshing way to ring in the holiday season.

Serving: 12 servings. | Prep: 15 m | Cook: 0 m | Ready in: 15 m

Ingredients

- 2 packages (3 ounces each) lime gelatin
- 2 cups boiling water
- 2 cans (15-1/4 ounces each) sliced or halved pears, drained
- 12 ounces whipped cream cheese
- 1 cup heavy whipping cream, whipped
- Leaf lettuce
- 6 maraschino cherries, halved

Direction

- In a bowl, dissolve gelatin in boiling water. Place pears in a blender or food processor; cover and process until smooth. Add cream cheese; process until smooth. Add to gelatin and stir well. Refrigerate until cool, about 15 minutes.
- Fold in whipped cream. Pour into 12 individual bell-shaped molds or other molds coated with cooking spray. Refrigerate until firm. Unmold onto lettuce-lined plates. Place a piece of cherry at the end of each bell for clapper.

Nutrition Information

- Calories: 242 calories
- Total Fat: 17g
- Cholesterol: 61mg
- Sodium: 157mg
- Total Carbohydrate: 21g
- Protein: 3g
- Fiber: 0 g

138. Luau Centerpiece

We couldn't wait to dig into this centerpiece at our Hawaiian Luau theme parties.--Carol Wakley, North East, Pennsylvania

Serving: 1 centerpiece. | Prep: 20 m | Cook: 0 m | Ready in: 20 m

Ingredients

- 4 packages (3 ounces each) berry blue gelatin
- 3 cups boiling water
- 3 cups cold water
- 2 medium unpeeled potatoes
- 4 medium carrots
- 4 medium green peppers
- Strawberries, grapes, and chunks of honeydew, cantaloupe, star fruit and pineapple
- 1 whole pineapple

Direction

- In a large bowl, dissolve gelatin in boiling water. Stir in cold water. Pour into an 8-cup ring mold coated with cooking spray. Refrigerate for 2 hours or until set.
- Cut each potato in half lengthwise for base of palm trees. Make a hole in the uncut side of potato halves that's large enough to hold a carrot; set aside. For tree trunks, use a sharp knife to make a thin petal-shaped cut on one side of each carrot toward the bottom, leaving slice attached. Rotate carrot a quarter turn and make another cut. Repeat one or two more times around carrot. Make another series of cuts about 1-1/2 in. above first set. Make a third series of cuts about 1-1/2 in. above second set. Insert carrots into potatoes.
- For palm leaves, cut tops off green peppers and remove seeds (discard tops or save for another use). Make deep V-shape cuts around bottom edge of pepper. Place a pepper on top of each carrot; secure with toothpicks.
- Thread fruit onto wooden skewers; insert into whole pineapple. Unmold gelatin ring and place on a 19-in. x 12-in. platter. Place whole pineapple in center of gelatin, and palm trees and any additional chunks of fruit around gelatin.

Nutrition Information

- Calories: 309 calories
- Total Fat: 0 g
- Cholesterol: 0 mg
- Sodium: 193mg
- Total Carbohydrate: 73g
- Protein: 8g
- Fiber: 0 g

139. Luncheon Mold

My mother served this many times at her bridge club when I was a child. It's now a favorite of my family on those hot summer days when a lighter meal is more appealing.

Serving: 6-8 servings. | Prep: 15 m | Cook: 0 m | Ready in: 15 m

Ingredients

- 1 package (3 ounces) lemon gelatin
- 1-1/3 cups boiling water
- 1/2 cup Miracle Whip
- 2 tablespoons prepared horseradish
- 1 teaspoon prepared mustard
- 2 cups chopped cooked corned beef
- 1 cup chopped celery
- 1/4 cup chopped green pepper
- 3 hard-boiled large eggs, chopped
- 2 tablespoons finely chopped onion
- Lettuce leaves, optional

Direction

- In a bowl, dissolve gelatin in boiling water; stir in Miracle Whip, horseradish and mustard. Chill until partially set; beat until foamy. Fold in corned beef, celery, green pepper, eggs and onion. Spoon into an oiled 4-cup mold. Chill until firm. Unmold onto a lettuce-lined platter if desired.

Nutrition Information

- Calories:
- Total Fat: g
- Cholesterol: mg
- Sodium: mg
- Total Carbohydrate: g
- Protein: g
- Fiber: g

140. Makeover Fluffy Lime Salad

Loaded with crunchy walnuts, tangy pineapple and lip-smacking lime flavor, this refreshing salad could even double as dessert! – Taste of Home Test Kitchen

Serving: 8 servings. | Prep: 10 m | Cook: 5 m | Ready in: 15 m

Ingredients

- 1 can (8 ounces) unsweetened crushed pineapple, undrained
- 1 package (.3 ounce) sugar-free lime gelatin
- 3 tablespoons water
- 6 ounces reduced-fat cream cheese
- 1 cup miniature marshmallows
- 1/2 cup chopped walnuts
- 1 carton (8 ounces) frozen reduced-fat whipped topping, thawed

Direction

- Drain pineapple, reserving juice; set pineapple aside. In a small saucepan, combine the gelatin, water and reserved juice. Cook and stir over low heat until gelatin is dissolved. Refrigerate until syrupy, about 30 minutes.
- In a small bowl, beat cream cheese until fluffy. Stir in gelatin mixture, marshmallows, walnuts and pineapple. Fold in whipped topping.
- Transfer to a serving bowl. Cover and refrigerate for 2 hours or until set.

Nutrition Information

- Calories: 206 calories
- Total Fat: 12g
- Cholesterol: 15mg
- Sodium: 125mg
- Total Carbohydrate: 21g
- Protein: 4g
- Fiber: 1g

141. Mango Delight Gelatin Mold

My son and I found this South American recipe while doing some research for a school project about Colombia. We made the dish as a visual aid for his project, and it was a hit!

Serving: 10 servings. | Prep: 30 m | Cook: 5 m | Ready in: 35 m

Ingredients

- 5 medium ripe mangoes, peeled and pitted
- 1 cup evaporated milk
- 3/4 cup sugar
- 1 cup orange juice
- 3 envelopes unflavored gelatin
- 2 cups whipped topping

Direction

- Cut the mangoes into large chunks; place in a food processor. Cover and process until smooth; transfer to a large bowl. Stir in milk and sugar; set aside.
- Place orange juice in a small saucepan; sprinkle gelatin over juice. Let stand for 2 minutes. Heat over low heat, stirring until gelatin is completely dissolved. Stir into mango mixture. Fold in whipped topping.
- Transfer to an 8-cup mold coated with cooking spray. Cover and refrigerate for 2 hours or until firm. Just before serving, unmold onto a serving platter.

Nutrition Information

- Calories:
- Total Fat: g
- Cholesterol: mg
- Sodium: mg
- Total Carbohydrate: g
- Protein: g
- Fiber: g

142. Mango Gelatin Salad

My Aunt Nannette shared this smooth and refreshing salad as a convenient do-ahead dish. The mango and apricot flavors go well with pork, chicken and beef. --Debra Sult, Chandler, Arizona

Serving: 8 servings. | Prep: 30 m | Cook: 0 m | Ready in: 30 m

Ingredients

- 2 cans (15 ounces each) diced or sliced mangoes, drained
- 1 package (8 ounces) cream cheese, softened and cubed
- 2 cups boiling water
- 2 packages (3 ounces each) lemon gelatin
- 1 package (3 ounces) apricot gelatin
- 2 cups cold water
- Fresh mint leaves and cranberries, optional

Direction

- Place mangoes and cream cheese in a food processor; process until blended.
- In a large bowl, add boiling water to gelatins; stir 2 minutes to completely dissolve. Stir in cold water, then mango mixture. Pour into an 8-cup ring mold coated with cooking spray or a 2-qt. serving bowl. Refrigerate until firm, about 4 hours. If using a ring mold, unmold onto a serving plate. If desired, serve with mint and cranberries.

Nutrition Information

- Calories: 227 calories
- Total Fat: 9g
- Cholesterol: 28mg
- Sodium: 147mg
- Total Carbohydrate: 35g
- Protein: 4g
- Fiber: 1g

143. Marshmallow Lime Salad

Cool, fluffy and green, this salad has lots of kid appeal despite the cottage cheese and mayonnaise mixed in it. My daughter enjoyed this salad as a child, and now her two children love it, too.--Fleda Collins, Talbott, Tennessee

Serving: 9-12 servings. | Prep: 10 m | Cook: 0 m | Ready in: 10 m

Ingredients

- 1 package (3 ounces) lime gelatin
- 1 package (3 ounces) lemon gelatin
- 2 cups boiling water
- 2 cups miniature marshmallows
- 1 can (20 ounces) crushed pineapple, undrained
- 1 cup (8 ounces) 4% cottage cheese
- 1 cup mayonnaise

Direction

- In a bowl, dissolve both packages of gelatin in boiling water. Add marshmallows and stir until dissolved. Chill until partially set.
- Combine the pineapple, cottage cheese and mayonnaise; stir into gelatin. Pour into a 9-in. square dish. Chill until firm.

Nutrition Information

- Calories: 259 calories
- Total Fat: 16g
- Cholesterol: 11mg
- Sodium: 200mg
- Total Carbohydrate: 27g
- Protein: 4g
- Fiber: 0 g

144. Mini Molded Salads

My homemaker club is proud to say we've never served a dish more than once at our monthly meetings. That's quite an accomplishment--considering we've been together 43 years! They're still talking about this one-of-a-kind salad. -- Delores Baumhofer, Montevideo, Minnesota

Serving: 7 servings. | Prep: 30 m | Cook: 0 m | Ready in: 30 m

Ingredients

- 2 packages (3 ounces each) lemon gelatin
- 2 cups boiling water
- 3 ounces cream cheese, softened
- 1 cup heavy whipping cream, divided
- 1 cup thinly sliced celery
- 1 cup sliced pimiento-stuffed olives
- SHRIMP SAUCE:
- 2 hard-boiled large eggs, finely chopped
- 1 cup mayonnaise
- 1 can (4 ounces) tiny shrimp, rinsed and drained
- 1 jar (2 ounces) chopped pimientos, drained
- 1/4 cup minced fresh parsley
- 2 tablespoons finely chopped onion
- 1 tablespoon lemon juice
- 1/2 teaspoon salt
- 1/4 teaspoon pepper

Direction

- In a bowl, dissolve gelatin in boiling water. Chill until syrupy, about 30 minutes. Meanwhile, beat cream cheese and 1 tablespoon cream in a bowl until smooth.
- In another bowl, beat remaining cream until soft peaks form; fold into cream cheese mixture. Fold in the celery, olives and gelatin. Pour into seven 6-oz. custard cups or molds coated with cooking spray; chill until firm.
- Combine sauce ingredients. Chill. Unmold salads onto individual plates. Serve with sauce.

Nutrition Information

- Calories: 557 calories
- Total Fat: 47g
- Cholesterol: 168mg
- Sodium: 1094mg
- Total Carbohydrate: 26g
- Protein: 9g
- Fiber: 1g

145. Minty Lime Gelatin

Crushed butter mints in this gelatin salad's topping lend a refreshing flavor to every bite. I make it for spring luncheons. --Eunice Stoen, Decorah, Iowa

Serving: 10-12 servings. | Prep: 10 m | Cook: 0 m | Ready in: 10 m

Ingredients

- 1 can (20 ounces) crushed pineapple, undrained
- 1 package (3 ounces) lime gelatin
- 1 package (10-1/2 ounces) miniature marshmallows
- 1 package (8 ounces) butter mints, finely crushed
- 1 cup heavy whipping cream, whipped

Direction

- Place pineapple with juice in a large bowl. Sprinkle with gelatin; stir until dissolved. Add marshmallows. Pour into a 13-in. x 9-in. dish. Chill for 6 hours or until set.
- In a bowl, fold butter mints into whipped cream, Spread over gelatin. Cut into squares.

Nutrition Information

- Calories: 277 calories
- Total Fat: 7g
- Cholesterol: 27mg
- Sodium: 67mg
- Total Carbohydrate: 52g
- Protein: 2g
- Fiber: 0 g

146. Missouri Peach and Applesauce Salad

"*Fresh peaches combine with applesauce in this tangy molded salad,*" notes Bernice Morris of Marshfield, Missouri about her creamy-textured, refreshing side dish.

Serving: 8-12 servings. | Prep: 20 m | Cook: 0 m | Ready in: 20 m

Ingredients

- 1 cup lemon-lime soda
- 1 package (3 ounces) peach or orange gelatin
- 1 cup applesauce
- 1 cup heavy whipping cream
- 1 tablespoon sugar
- 1/8 teaspoon ground nutmeg
- 1/8 teaspoon vanilla extract
- 1 cup chopped peeled ripe peaches
- Red grapes and mint leaves, optional

Direction

- In a saucepan, bring soda to a boil. Remove from the heat; stir in gelatin until dissolved. Add applesauce. Chill until mixture mounds slightly when dropped from a spoon.
- In a bowl, whip cream with sugar, nutmeg and vanilla until stiff. Fold into gelatin mixture along with the peaches. Transfer to a 1-1/2-qt. bowl. Chill until firm. Garnish with grapes and mint if desired.

Nutrition Information

- Calories: 121 calories
- Total Fat: 7g
- Cholesterol: 27mg
- Sodium: 26mg
- Total Carbohydrate: 14g
- Protein: 1g
- Fiber: 1g

147. Molded Asparagus Salad

We enjoy this salad in the spring with fried chicken. It's also good with turkey or chicken casseroles during winter. I even served it at Thanksgiving instead of a Waldorf salad. I began cooking when I was 8 years old. My parents did the farm chores before breakfast, so I decided I'd surprise them one morning by making biscuits while they were outside. I ended up with the dough on both hands that just wouldn't let loose--I can still see my mother's big grin when she came in and spotted me!

Serving: 6-8 servings. | Prep: 20 m | Cook: 0 m | Ready in: 20 m

Ingredients

- 1 cup sliced fresh asparagus
- 1 can (10-3/4 ounces) condensed cream of asparagus soup, undiluted
- 1 package (8 ounces) cream cheese, cubed
- 1 package (3 ounces) lemon gelatin
- 1 cup boiling water
- 1/2 teaspoon lemon extract
- 1/2 cup diced celery
- 1/2 cup diced green pepper
- 2 teaspoons finely chopped onion
- 2 teaspoons diced pimientos
- 1/2 cup finely chopped pecans
- 1/2 cup mayonnaise
- Celery leaves
- Chopped pimientos
- Lemon slice

Direction

- Cook asparagus in a small amount of water. Drain and set aside to cool. In a small saucepan, combine the soup and cream cheese over medium heat. Cook and stir until cheese is melted and mixture is blended.
- In a large bowl, dissolve gelatin in boiling water; add the extract. Cool. Add the asparagus, celery, green pepper, onion, diced pimientos, pecans, mayonnaise and soup mixture. Pour into 5- to 6-cup mold coated with nonstick cooking spray. Chill until firm, about 5 hours.
- Unmold; garnish with celery leaves, chopped pimientos and lemon slice.

Nutrition Information

- Calories: 320 calories
- Total Fat: 27g
- Cholesterol: 38mg
- Sodium: 421mg
- Total Carbohydrate: 16g
- Protein: 5g
- Fiber: 2g

148. Molded CherryPineapple Salad

I found this recipe in an area newspaper years ago. When this festive salad appears at a potluck, folks always come back for seconds...and sometimes thirds! I sometimes tint it with food coloring for the holidays.

Serving: 8-10 servings. | Prep: 15 m | Cook: 0 m | Ready in: 15 m

Ingredients

- 2 envelopes unflavored gelatin
- 1/4 cup cold water
- 1 can (20 ounces) crushed pineapple, undrained
- 1 package (8 ounces) cream cheese
- 1/2 cup sugar
- 2 tablespoons lemon juice
- 2 tablespoons maraschino cherry juice
- 1/2 pint heavy whipping cream, whipped
- 12 maraschino cherries, halved

Direction

- In a medium saucepan, dissolve gelatin in cold water. Add pineapple, cream cheese, sugar and juices; cook over medium heat, stirring often, until cream cheese is melted and gelatin is dissolved. Chill until syrupy. Fold in cream and cherries. Pour into an oiled 6-cup mold. Chill until firm.

Nutrition Information

- Calories: 253 calories

Nutrition Information

- Total Fat: 17g
- Cholesterol: 58mg
- Sodium: 80mg
- Total Carbohydrate: 24g
- Protein: 4g
- Fiber: 0 g

149. Molded Cranberry Fruit Salad

Instead of putting a bowl of plain cranberry sauce on the holiday table, I like to whip up this festive fruity salad. It adds pretty color to the meal.--Virginia Rexroat, Jenks, Oklahoma

Serving: 16 servings. | Prep: 15 m | Cook: 0 m | Ready in: 15 m

Ingredients

- 2 packages (.6 ounce each) sugar-free cherry gelatin
- 2 cups boiling water
- 1 package (12 ounces) fresh or frozen cranberries
- 1 large apple, peeled and chopped
- 1 large orange, peeled, chopped and seeded
- 1 piece of orange peel (1 inch)
- 1 can (20 ounces) crushed unsweetened pineapple, undrained

Direction

- In a bowl, dissolve gelatin in water. Stir in all remaining ingredients. Process in small batches in a blender until coarsely chopped. Pour into a 13-in. x 9-in. dish or a 3-qt. serving bowl. Chill until set, about 2-3 hours.

Nutrition Information

- Calories: 47 calories
- Total Fat: 1g
- Cholesterol: 0 mg
- Sodium: 46mg
- Total Carbohydrate: 11g
- Protein: 2g
- Fiber: 0 g

150. Molded Cranberry Gelatin Salad

To create this pretty salad mold, Jill combines the extra spiced cranberry sauce with fresh fruit, and some celery and nuts for crunch. "This dish is great with leftover turkey sandwiches," she remarks.

Serving: 8-10 servings. | Prep: 15 m | Cook: 20 m | Ready in: 35 m

Ingredients

- 2 envelopes unflavored gelatin
- 2-1/2 cups chilled cranberry juice
- 1 cup sugar
- 3 cups Sugar 'n' Spice Cranberries
- 1 small apple, peeled and finely chopped
- 1 medium navel orange, peeled and chopped
- 1/2 cup halved red seedless grapes
- 1/2 cup chopped walnuts, optional
- 1/4 cup finely chopped celery, optional

Direction

- In a large saucepan, sprinkle gelatin over the cranberry juice; let stand for 1 minute. Cook over low heat, stirring until gelatin is completely dissolved. Stir in sugar until dissolved. Add the cranberries, apple, orange, grapes, walnuts and celery if desired.
- Pour into an 8-cup ring mold coated with cooking spray. Refrigerate until set. Unmold onto a serving plate.

Nutrition Information

- Calories:
- Total Fat: g
- Cholesterol: mg
- Sodium: mg
- Total Carbohydrate: g
- Protein: g
- Fiber: g

151. Molded Cranberry Nut Salad

We try lots of cranberry recipes, and this one is always requested when we have family get-togethers at Thanksgiving and Christmas. It's also been a favorite dish at every church potluck I've taken it to! --Eleanor Arthur, Seattle, Washington

Serving: 10-12 servings. | Prep: 10 m | Cook: 10 m | Ready in: 20 m

Ingredients

- 1 envelope unflavored gelatin
- 1-1/2 cups cold water, divided
- 4 cups (16 ounces) fresh or frozen cranberries
- 1-1/2 cups sugar
- 1-1/2 cups dry red wine or cranberry juice
- 1 package (6 ounces) lemon gelatin
- 1-1/2 cups diced celery
- 3/4 cup chopped walnuts
- 1 cup sour cream
- 3/4 cup mayonnaise
- Celery leaves

Direction

- Soften unflavored gelatin in 1/2 cup water; set aside. In 3-qt. saucepan, combine cranberries, sugar and wine or cranberry juice; heat to boiling, stirring occasionally. Reduce heat and simmer 5 minutes, stirring frequently. Remove from heat. Add lemon gelatin and softened unflavored gelatin; stir until dissolved. Stir in remaining water. Chill until mixture is partially set. Fold in celery and walnuts. Pour into greased 8-cup mold; cover and chill until set. Meanwhile, combine sour cream and mayonnaise; refrigerate until ready to serve. To serve, unmold gelatin and top each serving with dollop of dressing. Garnish with celery leaves.

Nutrition Information

- Calories: 377 calories
- Total Fat: 19g
- Cholesterol: 18mg
- Sodium: 134mg
- Total Carbohydrate: 44g

- Protein: 5g
- Fiber: 2g

152. Molded Cranberry Salad

For 75 years, our parish, Christ Church, has served special luncheons. This fresh and fruity salad is one of my favorite recipes when cooking for a large group.--Shea Szachara, Binghamton, New York

Serving: 100 servings. | Prep: 20 m | Cook: 0 m | Ready in: 20 m

Ingredients

- 10 packages (6 ounces each) strawberry gelatin
- 5 quarts boiling water
- 10 cans (16 ounces each) whole-berry cranberry sauce
- 5 cups cold water
- 5 cans (20 ounces each) crushed pineapple, undrained
- 5 cans (15 ounces each) mandarin oranges, drained

Direction

- Dissolve gelatin in boiling water. Break up and stir in cranberry sauce until blended. Stir in cold water. Chill until partially set.
- Fold in pineapple with liquid and oranges. Coat five 13-in. x 9-in. pans with cooking spray; pour about 11-1/2 cups gelatin mixture into each. Chill until firm, about 4 hours.

Nutrition Information

- Calories: 19 calories
- Total Fat: 0 g
- Cholesterol: 0 mg
- Sodium: 5mg
- Total Carbohydrate: 5g
- Protein: 0 g
- Fiber: 0 g

153. Molded CranberryOrange Salad

I take this dish to potlucks during the holidays. People always ooh and aah. Feel free to sub whipped cream for the celery curl garnish. --Carol Mead, Los Alamos, New Mexico

Serving: 12 servings. | Prep: 20 m | Cook: 0 m | Ready in: 20 m

Ingredients

- 1 teaspoon unflavored gelatin
- 1 tablespoon plus 1 cup cold water, divided
- 1 cup boiling water
- 1 package (3 ounces) raspberry gelatin
- 3 cups (12 ounces) fresh or thawed frozen cranberries, divided
- 2 medium apples, cut into wedges
- 1 medium navel orange, peeled
- 1 cup sugar
- 1/2 cup chopped walnuts
- 1/2 cup finely chopped celery

Direction

- Sprinkle unflavored gelatin over 1 tablespoon cold water; let stand 1 minute. Add boiling water and raspberry gelatin; stir until gelatin is dissolved, about 2 minutes. Stir in remaining cold water. Refrigerate until thickened, about 45 minutes.
- Pulse 2-1/3 cups cranberries, apples and orange in a food processor until chopped. Transfer to a small bowl; stir in sugar. Stir fruit mixture into thickened gelatin. Fold in walnuts, celery and remaining whole cranberries.
- Coat a 10-in. fluted tube pan, an 8-cup ring mold or two 4-cup molds with cooking spray; pour in gelatin mixture. Cover and refrigerate overnight or until firm. Unmold onto a platter.

Nutrition Information

- Calories: 154 calories
- Total Fat: 3g
- Cholesterol: 0 mg
- Sodium: 21mg

- Total Carbohydrate: 32g
- Protein: 2g
- Fiber: 2g

154. Molded Egg Salad

Meet the Cook: Whenever I have company, I like to be able to just pop the food on the table. So this recipe's a real favorite of mine. I got it from a friend who made it for our church get-togethers. My husband and I raised four children; today, we have seven grandchildren. In our small town, farmland surrounds us on three sides, and we face the Columbia River on the other. -Lois Chapman, Ridgefield, Washington

Serving: 8-10 servings. | Prep: 15 m | Cook: 0 m | Ready in: 15 m

Ingredients

- 3 packets unflavored gelatin
- 1 cup water
- 2 cups mayonnaise
- 12 hard-boiled large eggs, chopped
- 1/2 cup chopped celery
- 1/2 cup chopped sweet red pepper
- 1/2 cup sliced green onions
- 1/2 cup sweet pickle relish
- 1 teaspoon salt
- 1/4 teaspoon pepper
- Thinly sliced fully cooked ham, optional

Direction

- In a medium saucepan, soften gelatin in water for 5 minutes. Stir over low heat until gelatin dissolves. Remove from the heat.
- Whisk in mayonnaise. Stir in eggs. Add celery, red pepper, onions, relish, salt and pepper; mix well. Pour into an 8-cup mold coated with cooking spray. Chill overnight.
- Unmold onto a serving platter. If desired, use ham as a garnish around the sides of the mold, or place several pieces in the center if using a ring mold.

Nutrition Information

- Calories: 441 calories
- Total Fat: 42g
- Cholesterol: 270mg
- Sodium: 660mg
- Total Carbohydrate: 6g
- Protein: 10g
- Fiber: 1g

155. Molded Peach Gelatin

For folks who don't care for cranberry sauce, consider serving this pleasant peach mold at your Thanksgiving dinner. It's convenient do-ahead dish when preparing for a busy day.

Serving: 4-6 servings. | Prep: 20 m | Cook: 0 m | Ready in: 20 m

Ingredients

- 1 can (15-1/4 ounces) sliced peaches
- 1/2 cup sugar
- 1/4 to 1/2 teaspoon ground nutmeg
- 1 package (3 ounces) peach or orange gelatin

Direction

- Drain peaches, reserving juice; add enough water to juice to measure 1 cup. Place peaches in a blender. Cover and process until smooth; set aside.
- In a large saucepan, combine the sugar, nutmeg and reserved juice mixture. Bring to a boil over medium heat; cook and stir for 1 minute or until sugar is dissolved. Remove from the heat; stir in gelatin until dissolved. Stir in the peach puree.
- Pour into a 3-cup mold coated with cooking spray. Refrigerate until set. Just before serving, unmold onto a serving plate.

Nutrition Information

- Calories: 173 calories
- Total Fat: 0 g

- Cholesterol: 0 mg
- Sodium: 38mg
- Total Carbohydrate: 43g
- Protein: 1g
- Fiber: 1g

156. Molded Rhubarb Salad

Says Sue Seymour of Valatie, New York, "My bright red salad sets fresh tart rhubarb in a fruity-sweet gelatin blend."

Serving: 10-12 servings. | Prep: 15 m | Cook: 0 m | Ready in: 15 m

Ingredients

- 3 cups diced rhubarb
- 2 cups water
- 1-2/3 cups sugar
- 1 package (6 ounces) strawberry gelatin
- 1 can (20 ounces) crushed pineapple, drained
- 1/2 cup chopped walnuts

Direction

- In a saucepan over medium heat, cook rhubarb in water until tender, about 5 minutes. Remove from the heat; stir in sugar and gelatin until dissolved. Add pineapple and nuts. Pour into an oiled 6-cup mold. Chill until set.

Nutrition Information

- Calories: 225 calories
- Total Fat: 3g
- Cholesterol: 0 mg
- Sodium: 34mg
- Total Carbohydrate: 49g
- Protein: 3g
- Fiber: 1g

157. Molded Strawberry Salad

This refreshing salad has two layers - a pretty pink bottom that includes sour cream, and a ruby red top with strawberries and pineapple. For years, Mom has included this salad in meals she prepares for our family. -Gloria Grant, Sterling, Illinois

Serving: 8 servings. | Prep: 10 m | Cook: 0 m | Ready in: 10 m

Ingredients

- 1 package (6 ounces) strawberry gelatin
- 1-1/2 cups boiling water
- 1 package (10 ounces) frozen sweetened sliced strawberries, thawed
- 1 can (8 ounces) unsweetened crushed pineapple
- 1 cup sour cream
- Leaf lettuce and fresh strawberries, optional

Direction

- In a large bowl, dissolve gelatin in water. Add strawberries and pineapple. Strain, reserving liquid and fruit. Set aside 1 cup of the liquid at room temperature.
- Pour fruit and remaining liquid into a 5-cup ring mold or 9-in. square pan that has been coated with cooking spray. Cover and refrigerate until set, about 1 hour.
- Whisk sour cream and reserved liquid; pour over top of gelatin. Cover and refrigerate until set.
- Cut into squares and place on individual plates; or unmold onto a serving platter. Garnish with lettuce and strawberries if desired.

Nutrition Information

- Calories: 182 calories
- Total Fat: 5g
- Cholesterol: 20mg
- Sodium: 64mg
- Total Carbohydrate: 31g
- Protein: 3g
- Fiber: 1g

158. Molded Vegetable Salad

I FOUND this recipe years ago in an old cookbook. By using different colored gelatins, it blends in well with special holiday dinners. Of course, I use lime for our St. Patrick's Day celebration. Whatever the holiday, this salad is a big hit and there's seldom any leftover. -Pauline Albert, Catasauqua, Pennsylvania

Serving: 8 servings. | Prep: 15 m | Cook: 0 m | Ready in: 15 m

Ingredients

- 1 package (6 ounces) lime gelatin
- 1/4 teaspoon salt, optional
- 1-1/2 cups boiling water
- 3/4 cup cold water
- 3 tablespoons vinegar
- 1 cup chopped celery
- 1 cup chopped tomato
- 1 cup thinly shredded lettuce
- 3/4 cup thinly sliced radishes
- 1/4 cup finely chopped green pepper
- 4 teaspoons grated onion
- Dash pepper

Direction

- In a bowl, dissolve gelatin and salt if desired in boiling water. Add the cold water and vinegar. Chill until partially set. Fold in remaining ingredients. Pour into a 4-cup mold that has been lightly coated with cooking spray. Chill until firm. Unmold onto a serving platter.

Nutrition Information

- Calories: 38 calories
- Total Fat: 0 g
- Cholesterol: 0 mg
- Sodium: 77mg
- Total Carbohydrate: 8g
- Protein: 2g
- Fiber: 0 g

159. Moms OrangeSpice Gelatin

I remember my mom making this tangy mold frequently when I was growing up. It was always one of our favorites. --Karen Grimes, Stephens City, Virginia

Serving: 10 servings. | Prep: 15 m | Cook: 10 m | Ready in: 25 m

Ingredients

- 1 can (15 ounces) sliced peaches in extra-light syrup
- 2 tablespoons cider vinegar
- 3 cinnamon sticks (3 inches)
- 12 whole cloves
- 3 cups boiling water
- 4 packages (.3 ounce each) sugar-free orange gelatin
- 2 cups cold water
- Sugar substitute equivalent to 1/3 cup sugar
- 1/4 cup finely chopped pecans

Direction

- Drain peaches, reserving syrup; set peaches aside. In a small saucepan, combine the vinegar, cinnamon sticks, cloves and reserved syrup. Bring to a boil; cook until reduced to about 1/2 cup. Strain, discarding cinnamon and cloves.
- Add boiling water to syrup mixture; stir in gelatin until dissolved. Stir in the cold water and sugar substitute. Refrigerate until slightly thickened, about 35 minutes.
- Coarsely chop the peaches. Stir peaches and pecans into gelatin mixture. Transfer to a 6-cup ring mold coated with cooking spray (mold will be full). Refrigerate for 3-4 hours or until firm. Unmold onto a serving plate.

Nutrition Information

- Calories: 62 calories
- Total Fat: 2g
- Cholesterol: 0 mg
- Sodium: 91mg

- Total Carbohydrate: 8g
- Protein: 2g
- Fiber: 1g

160. Orange Buttermilk Gelatin Salad

MY FAMILY loves this salad, and I do, too, because it's so easy to make! The buttermilk adds a wonderful tang, making it a refreshing accompaniment to any meal. -Lenore Wilson, Muskogee, Oklahoma

Serving: 10 servings. | Prep: 15 m | Cook: 0 m | Ready in: 15 m

Ingredients

- 1 can (20 ounces) crushed pineapple
- 1 package (6 ounces) orange gelatin
- 2 cups buttermilk
- 1 carton (8 ounces) frozen whipped topping, thawed

Direction

- In a saucepan, bring pineapple with juice to a boil. Stir in the gelatin until dissolved. Remove from the heat; stir in buttermilk. Cool to room temperature. Fold in whipped topping. Pour into an 11x7-in. dish or 2-qt. bowl. Chill for at least 4 hours.

Nutrition Information

- Calories: 115 calories
- Total Fat: 3g
- Cholesterol: 2mg
- Sodium: 93mg
- Total Carbohydrate: 16g
- Protein: 3g
- Fiber: 0 g

161. Orange Buttermilk Gelatin Salad Mold

A dear friend shared this recipe with me years ago. Now it's my favorite dish to take to a church meeting, shower or any potluck event--it's always a hit. Whenever I serve this salad, people ask for the recipe. They find it hard to believe it's really made with buttermilk! --Juanita Hutto, Mechanicsville, Virginia

Serving: 12-16 servings. | Prep: 15 m | Cook: 0 m | Ready in: 15 m

Ingredients

- 1 can (20 ounces) unsweetened crushed pineapple, undrained
- 3 tablespoons sugar
- 1 package (6 ounces) orange gelatin
- 2 cups buttermilk
- 1 carton (8 ounces) frozen whipped topping, thawed
- 1 cup chopped nuts

Direction

- In a saucepan, combine pineapple and sugar; bring to a boil, stirring occasionally. When mixture boils, immediately add gelatin and stir until dissolved. Cool slightly. Stir in buttermilk. Chill until partially set. Fold in whipped topping and nuts. If necessary, chill until mixture mounds slightly. Pour into a lightly oiled 8-1/2-cup mold. Chill overnight.

Nutrition Information

- Calories: 168 calories
- Total Fat: 7g
- Cholesterol: 1mg
- Sodium: 57mg
- Total Carbohydrate: 23g
- Protein: 4g
- Fiber: 1g

162. Orange Buttermilk Salad

For a deliciously creamy treat, I make this gelatin salad. It is so easy to whip up and I always receive compliments.-- Carol Van Sickle, Versailles, Kentucky

Serving: 12 servings. | Prep: 20 m | Cook: 0 m | Ready in: 20 m

Ingredients

- 1 can (20 ounces) crushed pineapple, undrained
- 1 package (6 ounces) orange gelatin
- 2 cups buttermilk
- 1 carton (8 ounces) frozen whipped topping, thawed

Direction

- In a saucepan, bring pineapple to a boil. Remove from the heat; add gelatin and stir to dissolve. Add buttermilk and mix well. Cool to room temperature. Fold in whipped topping. Pour into an 11x7-in. dish. Refrigerate several hours or overnight. Cut into squares.

Nutrition Information

- Calories: 157 calories
- Total Fat: 4g
- Cholesterol: 2mg
- Sodium: 76mg
- Total Carbohydrate: 28g
- Protein: 3g
- Fiber: 0 g

163. Orange Gelatin Cups

My mother used gelatin in so many good dishes, and as I got older, I did the same. This recipe is one I created. It's a refreshing accompaniment to any meal. -Mrs. John Eaton, Palm Harbor, Florida

Serving: 4 servings. | Prep: 5 m | Cook: 0 m | Ready in: 5 m

Ingredients

- 1 package (3 ounces) orange gelatin
- 1 cup boiling water
- 1 cup applesauce
- 1 can (11 ounces) mandarin oranges, drained

Direction

- In a small bowl, dissolve gelatin in boiling water. Stir in applesauce. Pour into four dessert dishes. Add oranges. Cover and refrigerate for 2 hours or until set.

Nutrition Information

- Calories: 151 calories
- Total Fat: 0 g
- Cholesterol: 0 mg
- Sodium: 54mg
- Total Carbohydrate: 38g
- Protein: 2g
- Fiber: 1g

164. Overnight Fruit Cup

I can't begin to count how many times I've been asked for this recipe...it's become my trademark! It's so simple because it's prepared the night before, giving me time to enjoy my mornings.

Serving: 15-20 servings. | Prep: 20 m | Cook: 0 m | Ready in: 20 m

Ingredients

- 1 package (3 ounces) lemon gelatin
- 2 cups boiling water

- 1 can (6 ounces) frozen orange juice concentrate, thawed
- 1 can (20 ounces) pineapple chunks, undrained
- 1 can (15-1/4 ounces) sliced peaches, drained
- 1 can (11 ounces) mandarin orange segments, undrained
- 1 cup sliced fresh strawberries
- 1 cup fresh blueberries
- 1 cup green grapes
- 1 firm banana, thinly sliced

Direction

- In a large bowl, dissolve gelatin in water. Add orange juice concentrate; mix well. Add all of the fruit; mix well. Cover and refrigerate overnight.

Nutrition Information

- Calories:
- Total Fat: g
- Cholesterol: mg
- Sodium: mg
- Total Carbohydrate: g
- Protein: g
- Fiber: g

165. Pastel Gelatin Salad

In Santee, California, Teresa Ries tops her gelatin salad with pretty pastel mini marshmallow to add color to holiday menus. With its creamy lemon-lime base and tangy pineapple flavor, it's a tasty accompaniment to any meal.

Serving: 15 servings. | Prep: 25 m | Cook: 0 m | Ready in: 25 m

Ingredients

- 1 package (3 ounces) lemon gelatin
- 1 package (3 ounces) lime gelatin
- 2 cups boiling water
- 1 package (8 ounces) cream cheese, cubed
- 1/2 cup evaporated milk
- 1/2 cup mayonnaise
- 1 can (8 ounces) unsweetened crushed pineapple, undrained

- 1/2 cup chopped walnuts
- 1 package (10-1/2 ounces) pastel miniature marshmallows

Direction

- In a large bowl, combine lemon and lime gelatin with boiling water; stir until dissolved. Add cream cheese; let stand for 10 minutes. Beat on high speed until smooth. Stir in milk and mayonnaise. Fold in pineapple.
- Pour into an ungreased 13-in. x 9-in. dish. Sprinkle with nuts and marshmallows. Cover and refrigerate until set.

Nutrition Information

- Calories: 250 calories
- Total Fat: 14g
- Cholesterol: 18mg
- Sodium: 135mg
- Total Carbohydrate: 30g
- Protein: 4g
- Fiber: 0 g

166. Patriotic Gelatin Salad

Almost as spectacular as the fireworks, this lovely salad makes quite a "bang" at our July Fourth meal. It's exciting to serve, and our guests loved the cool fruity and creamy layers. This salad really added to my patriotic theme. --Sue Gronholz, Beaver Dam, Wisconsin

Serving: 16 servings. | Prep: 20 m | Cook: 0 m | Ready in: 20 m

Ingredients

- 2 packages (3 ounces each) berry blue gelatin
- 2 packages (3 ounces each) strawberry gelatin
- 4 cups boiling water, divided
- 2-1/2 cups cold water, divided
- 2 envelopes unflavored gelatin
- 2 cups milk
- 1 cup sugar
- 2 cups sour cream
- 2 teaspoons vanilla extract

Direction

- In four separate bowls, dissolve each package of gelatin in 1 cup boiling water. Add 1/2 cup cold water to each and stir. Pour one bowl of blue gelatin into a 10-in. fluted tube pan coated with cooking spray; chill until almost set, about 30 minutes.
- Set other three bowls of gelatin aside at room temperature. Soften unflavored gelatin in remaining cold water; let stand 5 minutes.
- Heat milk in a saucepan over medium heat just below boiling. Stir in softened gelatin and sugar until sugar is dissolved. Remove from heat; stir in sour cream and vanilla until smooth. When blue gelatin in pan in almost set, carefully spoon 1-1/2 cups sour cream mixture over it. Chill until almost set, about 30 minutes.
- Carefully spoon one bowl of strawberry gelatin over cream layer. Chill until almost set. Carefully spoon 1-1/2 cups cream mixture over the strawberry layer. Chill until almost set. Repeat, adding layers of blue gelatin, cream mixture and strawberry gelatin, chilling in between each. Chill several hours or overnight.

Nutrition Information

- Calories: 69 calories
- Total Fat: 3g
- Cholesterol: 11mg
- Sodium: 84mg
- Total Carbohydrate: 5g
- Protein: 5g
- Fiber: 0 g

---

167. Peach Bavarian

Fruit molds are my specialty. This one, with its refreshing peach taste, makes a colorful salad or dessert. --Adeline Piscitelli, Sayreville, New Jersey

Serving: 8 servings. | Prep: 15 m | Cook: 0 m | Ready in: 15 m

Ingredients

- 1 can (15-1/4 ounces) sliced peaches
- 2 packages (3 ounces each) peach or apricot gelatin
- 1/2 cup sugar
- 2 cups boiling water
- 1 teaspoon almond extract
- 1 carton (8 ounces) frozen whipped topping, thawed
- Additional sliced peaches, optional

Direction

- Drain peaches, reserving 2/3 cup juice. Chop peaches into small pieces; set aside.
- In a large bowl, dissolve gelatin and sugar in boiling water. Stir in reserved syrup. Chill until slightly thickened. Stir extract into whipped topping; gently fold in gelatin mixture. Fold in peaches.
- Pour into an oiled 6-cup mold. Chill overnight. Unmold onto a serving platter; garnish with additional peaches if desired.

Nutrition Information

- Calories: 249 calories
- Total Fat: 5g
- Cholesterol: 0 mg
- Sodium: 53mg
- Total Carbohydrate: 47g
- Protein: 2g
- Fiber: 0 g

168. Peach Gelatin Salad

My mother always asked our family what we wanted to eat for holiday dinners. Without exception, our requests included this refreshing gelatin. Toasted walnuts give it a little crunch. --Dennis King, Navarre, Florida

Serving: 8 servings. | Prep: 15 m | Cook: 0 m | Ready in: 15 m

Ingredients

- 1 can (29 ounces) sliced peaches, drained
- 1-1/2 cups boiling water
- 2 packages (3 ounces each) lemon gelatin
- 1 can (12 ounces) ginger ale, chilled
- 1/3 cup chopped walnuts, toasted

Direction

- Arrange half of the peach slices in a 6-cup ring mold coated with cooking spray. In a small bowl, add boiling water to gelatin; stir 2 minutes to completely dissolve.
- Stir in ginger ale. Pour half of the mixture over peaches; sprinkle with walnuts. Refrigerate 30 minutes or until set but not firm. Let remaining gelatin mixture stand at room temperature.
- Carefully arrange remaining peach slices over gelatin in mold. Spoon remaining gelatin mixture over top. Refrigerate until firm. Unmold onto a serving plate.

Nutrition Information

- Calories:
- Total Fat: g
- Cholesterol: mg
- Sodium: mg
- Total Carbohydrate: g
- Protein: g
- Fiber: g

169. PeachCranberry Gelatin Salad

Harvest colors and flavors give this refreshing salad a delightful twist that's just right for Thanksgiving or any special meal. I use lime gelatin instead of peach for green and red salad at Christmastime. --Patty Kile, Elizabethtown, Pennsylvania.

Serving: 14-18 servings. | Prep: 20 m | Cook: 0 m | Ready in: 20 m

Ingredients

- 2 packages (3 ounces each) peach or orange gelatin
- 4 cups water, divided
- 1 cup orange juice
- 2 cans (15 ounces each) sliced peaches, drained
- 1 package (6 ounces) cranberry or raspberry gelatin
- 1 cup cranberry juice
- 2 large oranges, peeled
- 2 cups fresh or frozen cranberries
- 1 cup sugar

Direction

- Place peach gelatin in a large bowl. Bring 2 cups of water to a boil; pour over gelatin. Stir until dissolved. Add orange juice and mix well. Chill until partially set.
- Fold in peaches. Pour into a 3-qt. serving bowl. Chill until firm. Place cranberry gelatin in another bowl. Bring remaining water to a boil; pour over gelatin. Stir until dissolved. Add cranberry juice and mix well.
- In a food processor, combine the oranges, cranberries and sugar; process until the fruit is coarsely chopped. Add to the cranberry gelatin. Carefully spoon over gelatin. Chill until set.

Nutrition Information

- Calories:
- Total Fat: g
- Cholesterol: mg
- Sodium: mg
- Total Carbohydrate: g
- Protein: g

- Fiber: g

- Sodium: 82mg
- Total Carbohydrate: 37g
- Protein: 3g
- Fiber: 1g

170. Peaches n Cream Salad

Luscious fruit, cream cheese and gelatin come together to create an easy side dish for any occasion. The chopped pecans dotting the bottom layer provide a pleasing crunch for this satisfying salad. --Sue Braunschweig, Delafield, Wisconsin

Serving: 9 servings. | Prep: 15 m | Cook: 0 m | Ready in: 15 m

Ingredients

- 1 package (3 ounces) lemon gelatin
- 3/4 cup boiling water
- 1 cup orange juice
- 1 envelope whipped topping mix (Dream Whip)
- 3 ounces cream cheese, softened
- 1/4 cup chopped pecans, optional
- PEACH LAYER:
- 1 package (3 ounces) lemon gelatin
- 1 cup boiling water
- 1 can (21 ounces) peach pie filling

Direction

- In a bowl, dissolve gelatin in water; add orange juice. Refrigerate until partially set. Prepare topping mix according to package directions. In a bowl, beat cream cheese until smooth; fold in whipped topping and pecans if desired. Fold into gelatin mixture. Pour into an ungreased 8-in. square dish. Refrigerate until firm.
- For peach layer, dissolve gelatin in water; stir in pie filling. Chill until partially set. Carefully pour over creamy gelatin layer (pan will be full). Chill until firm.

Nutrition Information

- Calories: 198 calories
- Total Fat: 4g
- Cholesterol: 10mg

171. Peachy Applesauce Salad

I've been revising many recipes and creating new ones since my husband developed diabetes a couple of years ago. Folks will enjoy this dish whether it's served as a salad or dessert.--Marcille Meyer, Battle Creek, Nebraska

Serving: 6 servings. | Prep: 15 m | Cook: 0 m | Ready in: 15 m

Ingredients

- 1 cup diet lemon-lime soda
- 1 package (.3 ounces) sugar-free peach or mixed fruit gelatin
- 1 cup unsweetened applesauce
- 2 cups reduced-fat whipped topping
- 1/8 teaspoon ground nutmeg
- 1/8 teaspoon vanilla extract
- 1 fresh peach, peeled and chopped

Direction

- In a saucepan, bring soda to a boil. Remove from the heat; stir in gelatin until dissolved. Add applesauce; chill until partially set. Fold in whipped topping, nutmeg and vanilla. Fold in peach. Chill until firm.

Nutrition Information

- Calories: 99 calories
- Total Fat: 3g
- Cholesterol: 0 mg
- Sodium: 6mg
- Total Carbohydrate: 15g
- Protein: 0 g
- Fiber: 0 g

172. Pear Lime Gelatin

Packed with pears, this jolly gelatin salad is a light and refreshing treat. My Mom knew that fruit served in this fun form would get gobbled right up. She also liked it because the bowl looked like a sparkling jewel on our dinner table.

Serving: 6 servings. | Prep: 20 m | Cook: 0 m | Ready in: 20 m

Ingredients

- 1 can (29 ounces) pear halves in juice
- 1 package (3 ounces) lime gelatin
- 3 ounces cream cheese, cubed
- 1 cup whipped topping

Direction

- Drain pears, reserving juice; set pears and aside. Measure the juice; add water if needed to equal 1-1/2 cups. Pour into a saucepan; bring to a boil. Add gelatin; stir until dissolved. Gradually add cream cheese, whisking until smooth.
- Cover and refrigerate until cool. Mash reserved pears; fold into gelatin mixture. Fold in whipped topping. Pour into a 6-cup serving bowl. Refrigerate until set.

Nutrition Information

- Calories: 172 calories
- Total Fat: 3g
- Cholesterol: 5mg
- Sodium: 398mg
- Total Carbohydrate: 21g
- Protein: 8g
- Fiber: 2g

173. PearLime Gelatin Salad

A "must" at our family reunions is this easy make-ahead gelatin salad. Try decorating the top with maraschino cherries. The red and lime-green color is especially pretty for the holidays.

Serving: 8 servings. | Prep: 20 m | Cook: 0 m | Ready in: 20 m

Ingredients

- 1 can (15 ounces) pear halves
- 1 package (3 ounces) lime gelatin
- 1 package (8 ounces) cream cheese, cubed
- 1 can (20 ounces) unsweetened crushed pineapple, well drained
- 1 cup chopped pecans, toasted, divided
- 1 carton (8 ounces) frozen whipped topping, thawed

Direction

- Drain pears, reserving juice; set pears aside. In a small saucepan, bring juice to a boil. Stir in gelatin until dissolved. Remove from the heat; cool slightly.
- In a food processor, combine pears and cream cheese; cover and process until smooth. Transfer to a large bowl; stir in gelatin mixture until blended. Stir in the pineapple and 3/4 cup pecans. Fold in whipped topping.
- Pour into an ungreased 11x7-in. dish. Refrigerate until set. Sprinkle with remaining pecans. Cut into squares.

Nutrition Information

- Calories: 401 calories
- Total Fat: 25g
- Cholesterol: 31mg
- Sodium: 111mg
- Total Carbohydrate: 40g
- Protein: 5g
- Fiber: 3g

174. Picnic Potato Squares Salad

I'M ALWAYS on the lookout for new and unique recipes. Firm and cut into squares, this potato salad looks different than the usual ones, and the dill pickle gives it a unique flavor. It also travels well and is pretty served on salad greens. -Susan Furrow, Canterbury, New Brunswick

Serving: 9 servings. | Prep: 20 m | Cook: 0 m | Ready in: 20 m

Ingredients

- 2 envelopes unflavored gelatin
- 2-1/4 cups milk, divided
- 1 cup mayonnaise
- 1 tablespoon prepared mustard
- 2 teaspoons sugar
- 1/2 teaspoon salt
- 1/4 teaspoon pepper
- 2-1/2 cups cubed red potatoes, cooked and cooled
- 1/2 cup shredded carrot
- 1/2 cup thinly sliced celery
- 1/3 cup chopped dill pickle
- 2 tablespoons diced onion
- Lettuce leaves, optional

Direction

- Place the gelatin and 1 cup of milk in a saucepan; let stand for 1 minute. Cook and stir over low heat until gelatin is dissolved. Remove from the heat; stir in mayonnaise, mustard, sugar, salt, pepper and remaining milk until smooth. Chill until partially set. Fold in potatoes, carrot, celery, pickle and onion. Pour into an ungreased 8-in. square dish. Chill until firm. Cut into squares; serve on lettuce if desired.

Nutrition Information

- Calories: 261 calories
- Total Fat: 22g
- Cholesterol: 17mg
- Sodium: 394mg
- Total Carbohydrate: 12g
- Protein: 4g
- Fiber: 1g

175. Pina Colada Molded Salad

My gelatin ring gets a tropical twist from coconut, pineapple and macadamia nuts. It's a wonderful anytime treat. Now that I'm retired from teaching, I have more time for kitchen experiments. --Carol Gillespie, Chambersburg, Pennsylvania

Serving: 8 servings. | Prep: 25 m | Cook: 0 m | Ready in: 25 m

Ingredients

- 1 can (20 ounces) unsweetened crushed pineapple
- 2 envelopes unflavored gelatin
- 1/2 cup cold water
- 1 cup cream of coconut
- 1 cup (8 ounces) sour cream
- 3/4 cup lemon-lime soda
- 3/4 cup sweetened shredded coconut
- 1/2 cup chopped macadamia nuts
- Pineapple chunks and freshly shredded coconut, optional

Direction

- Drain pineapple, reserving juice; set the pineapple aside. In a large saucepan, sprinkle gelatin over cold water; let stand for 1 minute. Cook and stir over low heat until gelatin is completely dissolved, about 2 minutes.
- Remove from the heat; stir in the cream of coconut, sour cream, soda and reserved pineapple juice. Transfer to a large bowl. Cover and refrigerate for 30 minutes or until thickened, stirring occasionally.
- Fold in the flaked coconut, nuts and reserved pineapple. Pour into a 6-cup ring mold coated with cooking spray. Cover and refrigerate for 3 hours or until firm.
- To serve, unmold salad onto a platter. Fill the center with pineapple chunks and shredded coconut if desired.

Nutrition Information

- Calories: 331 calories
- Total Fat: 20g
- Cholesterol: 20mg
- Sodium: 82mg
- Total Carbohydrate: 37g
- Protein: 4g
- Fiber: 2g

176. Pineapple Citrus Gelatin Salad

Page Alexander of Baldwin City, Kansas notes, "We especially like this refreshing salad with barbecue."

Serving: 6 servings. | Prep: 15 m | Cook: 0 m | Ready in: 15 m

Ingredients

- 1 package (3 ounces) lemon gelatin
- 1 cup boiling water
- 1 can (8 ounces) crushed pineapple
- 1/3 cup orange juice concentrate
- 1 can (11 ounces) mandarin oranges, drained

Direction

- In a bowl, dissolve gelatin in boiling water. Drain pineapple, reserving juice. Set pineapple aside. Add enough water to the juice to equal 1 cup; stir into gelatin. Add orange juice concentrate. Chill until partially set. Fold in the pineapple and oranges. Pour into a 4-cup mold or glass bowl. Chill until set.

Nutrition Information

- Calories: 112 calories
- Total Fat: 0 g
- Cholesterol: 0 mg
- Sodium: 36mg
- Total Carbohydrate: 28g
- Protein: 2g
- Fiber: 1g

177. Pineapple Gelatin Salad

My family enjoys this lovely layered salad in the summer with grilled hamburgers. Although I haven't used the recipe long, it's quickly become a favorite. A good friend shared it with me, and every time I make it, I think of her. - Susan Kirby, Tipton, Indiana

Serving: 12-16 servings. | Prep: 25 m | Cook: 0 m | Ready in: 25 m

Ingredients

- 1 can (20 ounces) crushed pineapple
- 1 package (6 ounces) lemon gelatin
- 3 cups boiling water
- 1 package (8 ounces) cream cheese, softened
- 1 carton (16 ounces) frozen whipped topping, thawed
- 3/4 cup sugar
- 3 tablespoons lemon juice
- 3 tablespoons water
- 2 tablespoons all-purpose flour
- 2 large egg yolks, lightly beaten

Direction

- Drain pineapple, reserving juice. Dissolve gelatin in water; add pineapple. Pour into a 13-in. x 9-in. dish; chill until almost set, about 45 minutes.
- In a bowl, beat cream cheese and whipped topping until smooth. Carefully spread over gelatin; chill for 30 minutes. Meanwhile, in a saucepan over medium heat, combine sugar, lemon juice, water, flour, egg yolks and reserved pineapple juice; bring to a boil, stirring constantly. Cook 1 minute or until thickened. Cool. Carefully spread over cream cheese layer. Chill for at least 1 hour.

Nutrition Information

- Calories: 236 calories
- Total Fat: 10g
- Cholesterol: 42mg
- Sodium: 68mg
- Total Carbohydrate: 32g

- Protein: 3g
- Fiber: 0 g

- Protein: 5g
- Fiber: 2g

178. PineappleBlueberry Gelatin Salad

My husband has a green thumb, and our blueberry bushes are proof of his fruitful endeavors. This is one of our family's favorite blueberry dishes.

Serving: 8 servings. | Prep: 15 m | Cook: 0 m | Ready in: 15 m

Ingredients

- 2 packages (3 ounces each) grape gelatin
- 2 cups boiling water
- 1 can (20 ounces) crushed pineapple
- 2 cups fresh blueberries
- 1 package (8 ounces) cream cheese, softened
- 1/2 cup sour cream
- 1/2 cup sugar
- 1 teaspoon vanilla extract
- 1/2 cup chopped pecans

Direction

- In a large bowl, dissolve gelatin in boiling water. Drain pineapple, reserving juice in a measuring cup; add enough water to measure 1 cup. Stir into gelatin. Add pineapple and blueberries. Transfer to an 11x7-in. dish; cover and refrigerate until firm.
- In a small bowl, beat the cream cheese, sour cream, sugar and vanilla until smooth. Spread over gelatin. Cover and refrigerate until serving. Just before serving, sprinkle with pecans.

Nutrition Information

- Calories: 344 calories
- Total Fat: 18g
- Cholesterol: 41mg
- Sodium: 117mg
- Total Carbohydrate: 44g

179. PineappleLime Gelatin Mold

Jolly, jiggly gelatin comes in a rainbow of colors and fits any party mold! This lime-green salad from Christine Arter of Crestline, Ohio makes a refreshing and fun side dish.

Serving: 12 servings. | Prep: 10 m | Cook: 0 m | Ready in: 10 m

Ingredients

- 2 packages (3 ounces each) lime gelatin
- 2 cups boiling water
- 1 can (20 ounces) crushed pineapple, undrained
- 1 cup (8 ounces) sour cream
- 1/2 cup chopped pecans

Direction

- In a large bowl, dissolve gelatin in water. Stir in pineapple; cover and refrigerate until syrupy.
- Whisk in sour cream; add pecans. Transfer to a 6-cup ring mold coated with cooking spray. Cover and refrigerate until firm. Unmold onto a serving plate.

Nutrition Information

- Calories: 135 calories
- Total Fat: 7g
- Cholesterol: 13mg
- Sodium: 26mg
- Total Carbohydrate: 17g
- Protein: 2g
- Fiber: 1g

180. Pomegranate Gelatin

As a former home economics teacher, I like to surprise family and friends with recipes that are a little more special. This salad combines sweet and tart tastes. --Deidre Hobbs, Redding, California

Serving: 10 servings. | Prep: 15 m | Cook: 0 m | Ready in: 15 m

Ingredients

- 2 packages (3 ounces each) raspberry gelatin
- 2 cups boiling water
- 1 cup cold water
- 1-1/2 cups pomegranate seeds (about 2 pomegranates)
- 1 can (8 ounces) crushed pineapple, drained
- 1/2 cup sour cream
- 1/2 cup mayonnaise

Direction

- In a large bowl, dissolve gelatin in boiling water. Stir in cold water, pomegranate seeds and pineapple. Pour into an 11x7-in. dish. Refrigerate until firm.
- Combine sour cream and mayonnaise; spread over gelatin. Refrigerate until serving.

Nutrition Information

- Calories: 194 calories
- Total Fat: 11g
- Cholesterol: 12mg
- Sodium: 106mg
- Total Carbohydrate: 22g
- Protein: 2g
- Fiber: 0 g

181. Pomegranate Cranberry Salad

Juicy pomegranate seeds give cranberry gelatin a refreshing twist. For the crowning touch, top the salad with whipped topping and a sprinkling of pecans. --Lorie Mckinney, Marion, North Carolina

Serving: 8 servings. | Prep: 15 m | Cook: 0 m | Ready in: 15 m

Ingredients

- 1 package (.3 ounce) sugar-free cranberry gelatin
- 1 cup boiling water
- 1/2 cup cold water
- 1-2/3 cups pomegranate seeds
- 1 can (14 ounces) whole-berry cranberry sauce
- 1 can (8 ounces) unsweetened crushed pineapple, drained
- 3/4 cup chopped pecans
- Frozen whipped topping, thawed, optional
- Additional chopped pecans, optional

Direction

- In a large bowl, dissolve gelatin in boiling water. Add cold water; stir. Add the pomegranate seeds, cranberry sauce, pineapple and pecans. Pour into a 1-1/2-qt. serving bowl. Refrigerate for 4-5 hours or until firm. If desired, top with whipped topping and additional pecans.

Nutrition Information

- Calories: 190 calories
- Total Fat: 8g
- Cholesterol: 0 mg
- Sodium: 41mg
- Total Carbohydrate: 30g
- Protein: 2g
- Fiber: 2g

182. Pretty Gelatin Molds

Revive extra cranberry sauce in this good and easy salad. This is one of the recipes I made for the first Thanksgiving dinner I cooked years ago and has become a seasonal favorite at our house.--Dixie Terry, Goreville, Illinois

Serving: 4 servings. | Prep: 15 m | Cook: 0 m | Ready in: 15 m

Ingredients

- 1 package (3 ounces) orange gelatin
- 3/4 cup boiling water
- 3/4 cup whole-berry cranberry sauce
- 1 medium navel orange, peeled and finely chopped
- 4 lettuce leaves

Direction

- In a large bowl, dissolve gelatin in boiling water. Stir in cranberry sauce and orange. Pour into four 1/2-cup molds coated with cooking spray. Chill for 3-4 hours or until set. Unmold onto lettuce-lined plates.

Nutrition Information

- Calories: 93 calories
- Total Fat: 0 g
- Cholesterol: 0 mg
- Sodium: 49mg
- Total Carbohydrate: 22g
- Protein: 2g
- Fiber: 1g

183. Quick Cranberry Gelatin Salad

Since this tangy salad keeps well, I make it a day ahead for my Christmas menu. It's also a great choice to take to a holiday potluck - even people who aren't fond of cranberries think it's yummy. I got the recipe from a friend at church who likes to cook and bake as much as I do. -Betty Claycomb, Alverton, Pennsylvania

Serving: 8-10 servings. | Prep: 10 m | Cook: 0 m | Ready in: 10 m

Ingredients

- 1 package (6 ounces) cherry gelatin
- 1-1/2 cups boiling water
- 1 can (20 ounces) crushed pineapple, undrained
- 1 can (14 ounces) whole-berry cranberry sauce
- 1-1/2 cups seedless red grapes, halved
- 1/4 cup chopped pecans

Direction

- In a large bowl, dissolve gelatin in water. Stir in pineapple and cranberry sauce. Refrigerate for 30 minutes. Stir in grapes and pecans. Pour into a 2-qt. serving bowl. Refrigerate until firm.

Nutrition Information

- Calories: 146 calories
- Total Fat: 2g
- Cholesterol: 0 mg
- Sodium: 62mg
- Total Carbohydrate: 32g
- Protein: 1g
- Fiber: 0 g

184. Quick CranRaspberry Gelatin

This recipe is one of my favorites to make during the holiday season. Guests are delighted with the flavor.-- Colleen Sturma, Milwaukee, Wisconsin

Serving: 12 servings. | Prep: 20 m | Cook: 0 m | Ready in: 20 m

Ingredients

- 3 packages (3 ounces each) raspberry gelatin
- 2 cups boiling water
- 1 can (14 ounces) jellied cranberry sauce
- 1 can (21 ounces) raspberry pie filling
- 1 carton (8 ounces) frozen whipped topping, thawed

Direction

- In a large bowl, dissolve gelatin in boiling water. In a small bowl, whisk cranberry sauce; stir into gelatin mixture until blended. Refrigerate until partially set, about 1-1/2 hours.
- Fold in pie filling. Transfer to a 6-cup ring mold coated with cooking spray. Refrigerate for 4 hours or until set.
- Unmold onto a serving plate. Pipe whipped topping into center of ring.

Nutrition Information

- Calories: 228 calories
- Total Fat: 3g
- Cholesterol: 0 mg
- Sodium: 77mg
- Total Carbohydrate: 48g
- Protein: 2g
- Fiber: 2g

185. Rainbow Gelatin

Our kids love this salad's array of colors. The cool cream cheese layers complement the layers of gelatin.--Steve Mirro, Cape Coral, Florida

Serving: 16-20 servings. | Prep: 25 m | Cook: 0 m | Ready in: 25 m

Ingredients

- 6 packages (3 ounces each) fruit-flavored gelatins of your choice
- 6 cups boiling water, divided
- 3 cups cold water, divided
- 1 package (8 ounces) cream cheese, cut into six cubes

Direction

- In a bowl, dissolve one package of gelatin in 1 cup boiling water. Add 1/2 cup cold water; stir. Spoon half into an oiled 10-in. fluted tube pan. Chill until almost set, about 40 minutes. Cool the other half of gelatin mixture; pour into a blender. Add one cube of cream cheese and blend until smooth. Spoon over the first layer. Chill until set. Repeat five times, alternating plain gelatin layer with creamed gelatin layer, and chilling between each step. Just before serving, unmold onto a serving platter.

Nutrition Information

- Calories: 55 calories
- Total Fat: 4g
- Cholesterol: 12mg
- Sodium: 43mg
- Total Carbohydrate: 4g
- Protein: 1g
- Fiber: 0 g

186. Rainbow Gelatin Cubes

These perky gelatin cubes are fun to serve and to eat! I vary the colors to match the occasion - pink and blue for a baby shower, school colors for a graduation party, etc. Kids of all ages snap them up. -Deanna Pietrowicz, Bridgeport, Connecticut

Serving: about 9 dozen. | Prep: 30 m | Cook: 0 m | Ready in: 30 m

Ingredients

- 4 packages (3 ounces each) assorted flavored gelatin
- 6 envelopes unflavored gelatin, divided
- 5-3/4 cups boiling water, divided
- 1 can (14 ounces) sweetened condensed milk
- 1/4 cup cold water

Direction

- In a small bowl, combine one package flavored gelatin and one envelope unflavored gelatin. Stir in 1 cup boiling water until dissolved. Pour into a 13-in. x 9-in. dish coated with cooking spray; refrigerate until set but not firm, about 20 minutes.
- In small bowl, combine the condensed milk and 1 cup boiling water. In another bowl, sprinkle two envelopes unflavored gelatin over cold water; let stand for 1 minute. Stir in 3/4 cup boiling water. Add to milk mixture. Spoon 1 cup of the creamy gelatin mixture over the first flavored gelatin layer. Refrigerate until set but not firm, about 25 minutes.
- Repeat from beginning of recipe twice alternating flavored gelatin with creamy gelatin layers. Chill each layer until set but not firm before spooning next layer on top. Make final flavored gelatin; spoon over top. Refrigerate for at least 1 hour after completing last layer before cutting into 1-in. squares.

Nutrition Information

- Calories: 26 calories
- Total Fat: 0 g
- Cholesterol: 0 mg
- Sodium: 27mg

- Total Carbohydrate: 4g
- Protein: 2g
- Fiber: 0 g

187. Rainbow Gelatin Salad

This seven-layer gelatin salad will elicit oohs and aahs from all your guests. It's well worth the time it takes to prepare.

Serving: 16-20 servings. | Prep: 60 m | Cook: 0 m | Ready in: 60 m

Ingredients

- 7 packages (3 ounces each) assorted flavored gelatin
- 4-1/2 cups boiling water, divided
- 4-1/2 cups cold water, divided
- 1 can (12 ounces) evaporated milk, chilled, divided

Direction

- In a small bowl, dissolve one package of gelatin in 3/4 cup boiling water. Stir in 3/4 cup cold water. Pour into a 13-in. x 9-in. baking dish coated with cooking spray; refrigerate until firm, about 1 hour.
- Dissolve a second package of gelatin in 1/2 cup boiling water. Stir in 1/2 cup cold water and 1/2 cup milk. Spoon over the first layer. Chill until firm.
- Repeat five times, alternating with creamy gelatin. Chill until each layer is firm before adding the next layer. Refrigerate overnight. Cut into squares.

Nutrition Information

- Calories: 130 calories
- Total Fat: 1g
- Cholesterol: 5mg
- Sodium: 84mg
- Total Carbohydrate: 27g
- Protein: 4g
- Fiber: 0 g

188. Raspberry Congealed Salad

My sisters and I especially enjoyed Mom's cool tangy side dish, which looks so lovely on the table. The pineapple and raspberries are a delectable duo, and pecans add a hearty crunch. -Nancy Duty, Jacksonville, Florida

Serving: 6 servings. | Prep: 20 m | Cook: 0 m | Ready in: 20 m

Ingredients

- 1 can (8 ounces) crushed pineapple
- 1 package (12 ounces) frozen unsweetened raspberries, thawed
- 1 package (3 ounces) raspberry gelatin
- 1 cup applesauce
- 1/4 cup coarsely chopped pecans
- Mayonnaise, optional

Direction

- Drain pineapple and raspberries, reserving juices. Place fruit in a large bowl; set aside. Add enough water to the juice to measure 1 cup. Pour into a saucepan; bring to a boil. Remove from the heat; stir in gelatin until dissolved.
- Pour over fruit mixture. Add the applesauce and pecans. Pour into a 1-qt. bowl. Chill until set. Spoon into individual dessert dishes; top with a dollop of mayonnaise if desired.

Nutrition Information

- Calories: 151 calories
- Total Fat: 4g
- Cholesterol: 0 mg
- Sodium: 34mg
- Total Carbohydrate: 29g
- Protein: 3g
- Fiber: 3g

189. Raspberry Cranberry Gelatin Salad

This vibrant cranberry gelatin is great for a buffet. It's loaded with nuts, celery, raspberries and oranges.

Serving: 12-15 servings. | Prep: 30 m | Cook: 0 m | Ready in: 30 m

Ingredients

- 1 package (3 ounces) cranberry gelatin
- 1 package (3 ounces) cherry gelatin
- 1 package (3 ounces) raspberry gelatin
- 1 teaspoon ground cinnamon
- 1 can (8 ounces) crushed pineapple
- 3/4 cup each cherry, cranberry and orange juice
- 1 can (14 ounces) jellied cranberry sauce
- 1 cup red wine or grape juice
- 1 can (11 ounces) mandarin oranges, drained
- 1 package (10 ounces) frozen sweetened raspberries, thawed
- 1/2 cup finely chopped celery
- 1/2 cup chopped pecans or walnuts

Direction

- In a large bowl, combine gelatins and cinnamon; set aside. Drain pineapple, reserving juice; set pineapple aside.
- In a large saucepan, combine the cherry, cranberry and orange juices; add reserved pineapple juice. Bring to a boil. Pour over gelatin mixture; beat until dissolved.
- Stir in cranberry sauce and wine or grape juice until smooth. Stir in the oranges, raspberries, celery, nuts and pineapple. Pour into a 13-in. x 9-in. dish. Chill for 6 hours or overnight or until firm. Cut into squares.

Nutrition Information

- Calories: 206 calories
- Total Fat: 3g
- Cholesterol: 0 mg
- Sodium: 52mg
- Total Carbohydrate: 43g
- Protein: 2g
- Fiber: 2g

190. Raspberry Gelatin Jewels

Kids love this jiggly salad, and honestly, so do the adults. It's always going to be on my holiday buffet. --Brenda Leonard, APO, AP

Serving: 8 servings. | Prep: 10 m | Cook: 0 m | Ready in: 10 m

Ingredients

- 1 package (6 ounces) raspberry gelatin
- 1-1/2 cups boiling water
- 1 can (20 ounces) unsweetened crushed pineapple, drained
- 1 package (12 ounces) frozen unsweetened raspberries

Direction

- In a large bowl, dissolve gelatin in boiling water. Stir in fruit. Pour into a greased 11x7-in. dish. Refrigerate for 4 hours or until firm. Cut into squares.

Nutrition Information

- Calories: 139 calories
- Total Fat: 0 g
- Cholesterol: 0 mg
- Sodium: 50mg
- Total Carbohydrate: 34g
- Protein: 3g
- Fiber: 2g

191. Raspberry Gelatin Salad

"We had an annual potluck at work," relates Pat Squire of Alexandria, Virginia. "Wonderful recipes came out of that meal - this cool, tart gelatin salad is one. I'm diabetic, and when I'm asked to share a dish, this is what I take."

Serving: 15 servings. | Prep: 10 m | Cook: 0 m | Ready in: 10 m

Ingredients

- 3 packages (.3 ounce each) sugar-free raspberry gelatin
- 1-1/2 cups boiling water
- 1 package (12 ounces) frozen unsweetened raspberries
- 1 can (20 ounces) unsweetened pineapple, undrained
- 2 medium ripe bananas, mashed
- 1 cup fat-free sour cream

Direction

- In a bowl, dissolve gelatin in water. Stir in raspberries, pineapple and bananas. Pour half into an 11x7-in. dish; refrigerate for 30 minutes or until firm. Set aside the remaining gelatin mixture at room temperature. Spread sour cream over gelatin in pan; top with remaining gelatin mixture. Refrigerate for 1 hour or until firm.

Nutrition Information

- Calories: 63 calories
- Total Fat: 0 g
- Cholesterol: 1mg
- Sodium: 50mg
- Total Carbohydrate: 14g
- Protein: 2g
- Fiber: 0 g

192. Raspberry Luscious Gelatin Salad

For a delicious refreshing summer salad, try this recipe. The sweetness of the pineapple and raspberry are perfect together.--Bonnie Barclay, Custer, Michigan

Serving: 16 servings. | Prep: 20 m | Cook: 0 m | Ready in: 20 m

Ingredients

- 2 packages (3 ounces each) raspberry gelatin
- 1 envelope unflavored gelatin
- 1 cup boiling water
- 2 cups cold water
- 1 can (20 ounces) crushed pineapple with juice
- 2 large ripe bananas, mashed
- 1 pint fresh or frozen whole unsweetened raspberries
- 1 cup sour cream

Direction

- In large bowl, combine raspberry gelatin, unflavored gelatin and boiling water; stir until dissolved. Stir in the cold water, then pineapple, bananas and raspberries.
- Pour half of gelatin mixture into glass serving bowl or 13x9-in. dish; chill until firm. (Let remaining half stand at room temperature.), When gelatin is firm, spread sour cream evenly over top, then carefully spoon reserved mixture over the sour cream. Chill until firm.

Nutrition Information

- Calories: 102 calories
- Total Fat: 3g
- Cholesterol: 10mg
- Sodium: 21mg
- Total Carbohydrate: 18g
- Protein: 2g
- Fiber: 2g

193. Red White and Blueberry Salad

Lovely and layered, this delightful gelatin salad rounds out any meal fruitfully. "Originally my grandmother's recipe. I regularly make it for potlucks," details. Linnea Tucker of Dolores, Colorado. "I believe my father would eat the entire dish himself it I let him!"

Serving: 12-16 servings. | Prep: 30 m | Cook: 0 m | Ready in: 30 m

Ingredients

- 2 packages (3 ounces each) raspberry gelatin
- 2 cups boiling water, divided
- 1-1/2 cups cold water, divided
- 1 envelope unflavored gelatin
- 1 cup half-and-half cream
- 3/4 to 1 cup sugar
- 1 package (8 ounces) cream cheese, cubed
- 1/2 cup chopped pecans
- 1 teaspoon vanilla extract
- 1 can (15 ounces) blueberries in syrup, undrained

Direction

- In a large bowl, dissolve one package of raspberry gelatin in 1 cup boiling water. Stir in 1 cup cold water. Pour into a 13-in. x 9-in. dish; chill until set. In a small bowl, soften unflavored gelatin in the remaining cold water; set aside.
- In a large saucepan, combine cream and sugar; whisk over medium heat until sugar is dissolved. Add cream cheese and softened unflavored gelatin; cook and stir until smooth. Cool. Stir in pecans and vanilla. Spoon over raspberry gelatin. Refrigerate until completely set.
- In a large bowl, dissolve second package of raspberry gelatin in remaining boiling water. Stir in blueberries. Carefully spoon over cream cheese layer. Chill several hours or overnight.

Nutrition Information

- Calories:
- Total Fat: g

- Cholesterol: mg
- Sodium: mg
- Total Carbohydrate: g
- Protein: g
- Fiber: g

194. Red White n Blue Salad

Our striking "flag" salad drew plenty of attention at our Independence Day party. The shimmering stripes are formed with distinctive gelatin layers. It makes you want to salute before spooning some up! —Laurie Neverman, Green Bay, Wisconsin

Serving: 16 servings. | Prep: 30 m | Cook: 0 m | Ready in: 30 m

Ingredients

- 1 package (3 ounces) berry blue gelatin
- 2 cups boiling water, divided
- 2-1/2 cups cold water, divided
- 1 cup fresh blueberries
- 1 envelope unflavored gelatin
- 1 cup heavy whipping cream
- 6 tablespoons sugar
- 2 cups sour cream
- 1 teaspoon vanilla extract
- 1 package (3 ounces) raspberry gelatin
- 1 cup fresh raspberries
- Whipped topping and additional berries, optional

Direction

- Dissolve berry blue gelatin in 1 cup boiling water; stir in 1 cup cold water. Add blueberries. Pour into a 3-qt. serving bowl. Refrigerate until firm, about 1 hour.
- In a saucepan, sprinkle unflavored gelatin over 1/2 cup cold water; let stand for 1 minute. Add cream and sugar; cook and stir over low heat until dissolved. Cool to room temperature. Whisk in sour cream and vanilla. Spoon over blue layer. Refrigerate until firm.
- Dissolve raspberry gelatin in remaining hot water; stir in remaining cold water. Add raspberries. Spoon over cream layer. Chill

until set. Top with whipped topping and berries if desired.

Nutrition Information

- Calories: 179 calories
- Total Fat: 11g
- Cholesterol: 40mg
- Sodium: 46mg
- Total Carbohydrate: 18g
- Protein: 3g
- Fiber: 1g

195. RedHot Gelatin Salad

"This is my grandma's recipe," writes Paula Ptomey of Porterville, California. "My mother makes this salad just about every year during the holidays. It has a spicy cinnamon taste that is really good. Even my daughter, who is a picky eater, likes it."

Serving: 6 servings. | Prep: 15 m | Cook: 0 m | Ready in: 15 m

Ingredients

- 1 package (3 ounces) cherry gelatin
- 1-1/2 cups boiling water, divided
- 1/4 cup red-hot candies
- 1/4 cup plus 1-1/2 teaspoons cold water
- 1 cup chopped tart apples
- 1 cup chopped celery
- 1/2 cup chopped walnuts

Direction

- In a small bowl, dissolve gelatin in 1 cup boiling water. In another bowl, dissolve red-hots in remaining water; stir into gelatin. Stir in cold water. Refrigerate until slightly thickened, about 1 hour.
- Fold in the apples, celery and walnuts. Pour into a 4-cup mold coated with cooking spray. Refrigerate for 2 hours or until firm.

Nutrition Information

- Calories:

- Total Fat: g
- Cholesterol: mg
- Sodium: mg
- Total Carbohydrate: g
- Protein: g
- Fiber: g

196. RedHot Molded Hearts

This cool salad gets a bit of "warmth" from melted cinnamon candies. Stirred into strawberry gelatin, the applesauce picks up a rosy hue and molds wonderfully. -- Kay Curtis, Guthrie, Oklahoma

Serving: 10-12 servings. | Prep: 15 m | Cook: 0 m | Ready in: 15 m

Ingredients

- 1/4 cup red-hot candies
- 1 cup boiling water
- 1 package (3 ounces) strawberry gelatin
- 2-1/2 cups applesauce

Direction

- In a large bowl, dissolve candies in water. Stir in gelatin until dissolved. Fold in applesauce. Pour into twelve greased 1/3-cup individual molds, a 4-cup heart-shaped mold or a 1-qt. bowl. Refrigerate overnight or until set.

Nutrition Information

- Calories:
- Total Fat: g
- Cholesterol: mg
- Sodium: mg
- Total Carbohydrate: g
- Protein: g
- Fiber: g

197. RedWhiteandBlue Berry Delight

Loaded with fresh strawberries and blueberries, this luscious JELL-O is perfect for any Fourth of July celebration! --Constance Fennell, Grand Junction, Michigan

Serving: 8 servings. | Prep: 20 m | Cook: 5 m | Ready in: 25 m

Ingredients

- 1/2 cup sugar
- 2 envelopes unflavored gelatin
- 4 cups white cranberry-peach juice drink, divided
- 1 tablespoon lemon juice
- 2 cups fresh strawberries, halved
- 2 cups fresh blueberries
- CREAM:
- 1/2 cup heavy whipping cream
- 1 tablespoon sugar
- 1/4 teaspoon vanilla extract

Direction

- In a large saucepan, combine sugar and gelatin. Add 1 cup cranberry-peach juice; cook and stir over low heat until gelatin is completely dissolved, about 5 minutes. Remove from the heat; stir in lemon juice and remaining cranberry-peach juice.
- Place strawberries in an 8-cup ring mold coated with cooking spray; add 2 cups gelatin mixture. Refrigerate until set but not firm, about 30 minutes. Set aside remaining gelatin mixture.
- Stir blueberries into remaining gelatin mixture; spoon over strawberry layer. Refrigerate overnight. Unmold onto a serving platter.
- In a small bowl, beat cream until it begins to thicken. Add sugar and vanilla; beat until stiff peaks form. Serve with gelatin.

Nutrition Information

- Calories: 203 calories
- Total Fat: 6g

- Cholesterol: 20mg
- Sodium: 12mg
- Total Carbohydrate: 38g
- Protein: 3g
- Fiber: 2g

198. Refreshing Rhubarb Salad

Nearly everyone I know has rhubarb in their garden, so it is indeed plentiful each spring. I've had this recipe in my scrapbook for years and serve it often at potlucks.

Serving: 12-14 servings. | Prep: 20 m | Cook: 0 m | Ready in: 20 m

Ingredients

- 4 cups diced fresh or frozen rhubarb
- 1-1/2 cups water
- 1/2 cup sugar
- 1 package (6 ounces) strawberry gelatin
- 1 cup orange juice
- 1 teaspoon grated orange zest
- 1 cup sliced fresh strawberries
- Mayonnaise, fresh mint and additional strawberries, optional

Direction

- In a saucepan over medium heat, bring the rhubarb, water and sugar to a boil. Cook, uncovered, until rhubarb is tender, about 6-8 minutes. Remove from the heat; stir in gelatin until dissolved. Stir in the orange juice and zest.
- Chill until mixture begins to thicken. Fold in strawberries. Pour into a 2-qt. bowl; chill until set. If desired, garnish with a dollop of mayonnaise, mint and strawberries.

Nutrition Information

- Calories: 91 calories
- Total Fat: 0 g
- Cholesterol: 0 mg
- Sodium: 29mg
- Total Carbohydrate: 22g

- Protein: 2g
- Fiber: 1g

199. Rhubarb Berry Delight Salad

This recipe will be an instant success. This layered gelatin dish does take some time to prepare but it is worth the work.--Joan Sieck, Rensselaer, New York

Serving: 12 servings. | Prep: 30 m | Cook: 0 m | Ready in: 30 m

Ingredients

- 4 cups diced fresh rhubarb or frozen rhubarb
- 2 cups fresh or frozen strawberries
- 1-1/2 cups sugar, divided
- 1 package (6 ounces) raspberry gelatin
- 2 cups boiling water
- 1 cup milk
- 1 envelope unflavored gelatin
- 1/4 cup cold water
- 1-1/2 teaspoons vanilla extract
- 2 cups sour cream

Direction

- In a large saucepan, cook rhubarb, strawberries and 1 cup sugar until fruit is tender. In a large bowl, dissolve raspberry gelatin in boiling water. Stir in fruit; set aside.
- In another saucepan, heat milk and remaining sugar over low until sugar is dissolved. Meanwhile, soften unflavored gelatin in cold water. Add to hot milk mixture and stir until gelatin dissolves. Remove from the heat; add vanilla. Cool to lukewarm; blend in sour cream. Set aside at room temperature.
- Pour a third of the fruit mixture into a 3-qt. bowl; chill until almost set. Spoon a third of the sour cream mixture over fruit; chill until almost set. Repeat layers twice, chilling between layers if necessary. Refrigerate until firm, at least 3 hours.

Nutrition Information

- Calories: 255 calories
- Total Fat: 7g
- Cholesterol: 28mg
- Sodium: 64mg
- Total Carbohydrate: 43g
- Protein: 4g
- Fiber: 1g

Nutrition Information

- Calories: 204 calories
- Total Fat: 0 g
- Cholesterol: 0 mg
- Sodium: 73mg
- Total Carbohydrate: 50g
- Protein: 3g
- Fiber: 1g

200. Rhubarb Pear Gelatin

Rhubarb season is almost here...and this is one of my family's favorite ways to eat it. I tried this mixture of ingredients on my own, and my family of 12 couldn't get enough. --Linda Strubhar, Cataldo, Idaho

Serving: 12 servings. | Prep: 15 m | Cook: 10 m | Ready in: 25 m

Ingredients

- 2 packages (6 ounces each) strawberry gelatin
- 2 cups miniature marshmallows, divided
- 4 cups sliced fresh or frozen rhubarb
- 2 cups water
- 2/3 cup sugar
- 2 cups cold water
- 1 can (15-1/4 ounces) sliced pears, drained and chopped

Direction

- Place gelatin and 1 cup marshmallows in a large bowl; set aside.
- In a large saucepan, combine the rhubarb, water and sugar. Bring to a boil. Reduce heat; cover and simmer for 3-4 minutes or until rhubarb is tender. Remove from the heat; pour over marshmallow mixture, stirring to dissolve gelatin. Stir in the cold water, pears and remaining marshmallows.
- Transfer to a 13-in. x 9-in. dish. Refrigerate for at least 6 hours or until firm.

201. RhubarbStrawberry Gelatin Molds

"This recipe comes from a neighbor with a very large and beautiful rhubarb and strawberry patch," says Janice Wiebelt from Hartville, Ohio. "This was her favorite salad and one of mine as well!"

Serving: 2 servings. | Prep: 15 m | Cook: 0 m | Ready in: 15 m

Ingredients

- 1 cup diced fresh or frozen rhubarb
- 1/4 cup water
- 1 tablespoon sugar
- 3 tablespoons plus 1 teaspoon strawberry gelatin
- 1/4 cup sliced fresh strawberries
- 1/4 cup orange juice
- 1/4 teaspoon grated orange zest
- Whipped cream, optional

Direction

- In a small saucepan over medium heat, bring the rhubarb, water and sugar to a boil. Reduce heat; simmer, uncovered, for 3-5 minutes or until rhubarb is tender. Remove from the heat; stir in gelatin until dissolved. Add the strawberries, orange juice and zest.
- Divide between two 4-in. mini fluted pans coated with cooking spray; refrigerate for 4 hours or until firm. Just before serving, invert molds onto serving plates; garnish with whipped cream if desired.

Nutrition Information

- Calories: 143 calories
- Total Fat: 0 g
- Cholesterol: 0 mg
- Sodium: 56mg
- Total Carbohydrate: 34g
- Protein: 3g
- Fiber: 2g

202. Rosey Raspberry Salad

Whenever I make this pretty raspberry salad, people talk! It's a festive side dish that works well for celebrations throughout the year. --Jane Vanderground, Macedonia, Ohio

Serving: 12-14 servings. | Prep: 15 m | Cook: 0 m | Ready in: 15 m

Ingredients

- 3 packages (3 ounces each) raspberry gelatin
- 3 cups boiling water
- 3 cups raspberry sherbet
- 1 package (12 ounces) unsweetened frozen raspberries

Direction

- In a large bowl, dissolve gelatin in boiling water. Add sherbet and stir until melted. Chill until syrupy. Add raspberries. Pour into an oiled 8-cup mold. Chill until firm.

Nutrition Information

- Calories: 77 calories
- Total Fat: 1g
- Cholesterol: 2mg
- Sodium: 29mg
- Total Carbohydrate: 17g
- Protein: 1g
- Fiber: 1g

203. Rosy Rhubarb Mold

This mold is perfect for a buffet. This recipe will feed a crowd with no problem at all.--Taste of Home Test Kitchen, Greendale, Wisconsin

Serving: 50 servings. | Prep: 40 m | Cook: 0 m | Ready in: 40 m

Ingredients

- 24 cups chopped rhubarb
- 6 cups water
- 3 cups sugar
- 6 packages (6 ounces each) strawberry gelatin
- 3 cups orange juice
- 2 tablespoons grated orange zest
- 6 cups sliced fresh strawberries
- Leaf lettuce
- Additional strawberries
- DRESSING:
- 3 cups mayonnaise
- 3 cups whipped topping
- 6 to 7 tablespoons whole milk

Direction

- In a kettle over medium-low heat, cook and stir rhubarb, water and sugar until rhubarb is soft and tender. Remove from the heat; stir in gelatin until dissolved. Stir in orange juice and zest. Chill until partially set, about 2-3 hours. Stir in strawberries. Pour into six 5-cup ring molds coated with cooking spray. Refrigerate overnight. Unmold onto lettuce-line platters; garnish with berries.
- For dressing, combine mayonnaise and whipped topping; add enough milk to thin to desired consistency. Serve in a bowl in center of mold.

Nutrition Information

- Calories: 193 calories
- Total Fat: 12g
- Cholesterol: 5mg
- Sodium: 83mg
- Total Carbohydrate: 22g
- Protein: 1g
- Fiber: 2g

204. Rosy Rhubarb Salad

This is one of my favorite springtime recipes. But if you freeze strawberries and rhubarb, you can make this salad most any time of year. You'll find it a little tart, and light and cool - just right for those warmer days ahead.

Serving: 8-10 servings. | Prep: 25 m | Cook: 0 m | Ready in: 25 m

Ingredients

- 4 cups diced raw or frozen rhubarb
- 1/2 cup water
- 1/2 cup sugar
- 2 packages (3 ounces each) strawberry gelatin
- 1 cup applesauce
- 1 cup orange juice
- 2 teaspoons grated orange zest
- 1 cup sliced fresh strawberries

Direction

- In a saucepan, combine rhubarb, water and sugar. Cook over medium heat until rhubarb is tender. In a large bowl, combine hot rhubarb and gelatin. Stir until dissolved. Add applesauce, orange juice and peel. Chill until syrupy. Fold in strawberries. Pour into a lightly greased 5-6 cup mold. Chill until set, about 4 hours or overnight.

Nutrition Information

- Calories: 107 calories
- Total Fat: 0 g
- Cholesterol: 0 mg
- Sodium: 22mg
- Total Carbohydrate: 26g
- Protein: 1g
- Fiber: 2g

205. Ruby Apple Salad

This is a pretty salad and tastes good, too. There are 22 apple growers in the county where I live, so I have plenty of fresh apples to use for cooking. Years ago, there used to be local apple contests that my two children and I would enter. One year we made a clean sweep of the awards - and I believe this recipe was one of the winners!

Serving: 6-8 servings. | Prep: 10 m | Cook: 0 m | Ready in: 10 m

Ingredients

- 1 package (3 ounces) cherry gelatin
- 2 tablespoons red-hot candies
- 1-3/4 cups boiling water
- 1-1/2 to 2 cups chopped apples
- 1/2 cup chopped celery
- 1/2 cup chopped walnuts

Direction

- In a bowl, stir gelatin and candies in boiling water until dissolved. Chill until partially set. Fold in apples, celery and walnuts. Pour into a 1-qt. serving bowl. Chill until firm, at least 4 hours.

Nutrition Information

- Calories:
- Total Fat: g
- Cholesterol: mg
- Sodium: mg
- Total Carbohydrate: g
- Protein: g
- Fiber: g

206. Ruby Gelatin Salad

I remember when I was a child that my older siblings and I didn't care for cranberry sauce. So every Thanksgiving, Mom would fix this gelatin salad just for us, and we would devour it.

Serving: 8 servings. | Prep: 10 m | Cook: 0 m | Ready in: 10 m

Ingredients

- 1 package (3 ounces) cherry gelatin
- 1 cup boiling water
- 1 cup orange juice
- 1 cup diced peeled apple
- 1 cup chopped celery
- 1/2 cup chopped walnuts

Direction

- In a bowl, dissolve gelatin in water. Add orange juice; refrigerate until partially set. Stir in apple, celery and walnuts. Refrigerate until firm.

Nutrition Information

- Calories: 72 calories
- Total Fat: 5g
- Cholesterol: 0 mg
- Sodium: 13mg
- Total Carbohydrate: 7g
- Protein: 2g
- Fiber: 0 g

207. Ruby Red Raspberry Salad

A refreshing and attractive side dish, this salad adds a festive touch to your holiday table. Children especially like this slightly sweet salad. -Marge Clark, West Lebanon, Indiana

Serving: 12-16 servings. | Prep: 15 m | Cook: 0 m | Ready in: 15 m

Ingredients

- 1 package (3 ounces) raspberry gelatin
- 2 cups boiling water, divided
- 1 package (10 ounces) frozen sweetened raspberries
- 1-1/2 cups sour cream
- 1 package (3 ounces) cherry gelatin
- 1 can (20 ounces) crushed pineapple, drained
- 1 can (14 ounces) whole-berry cranberry sauce
- Mayonnaise and mint sprigs, optional

Direction

- Dissolve raspberry gelatin in 1 cup boiling water. Add raspberries and stir until berries are thawed and separated. Pour into a 13-in. x 9-in. dish; chill until set.
- Carefully spread with sour cream; chill. Dissolve cherry gelatin in remaining boiling water. Add pineapple and cranberry sauce; mix well. Allow to thicken slightly.
- Carefully spoon over sour cream mixture; chill. If desired, garnish with mayonnaise and mint.

Nutrition Information

- Calories: 164 calories
- Total Fat: 4g
- Cholesterol: 15mg
- Sodium: 42mg
- Total Carbohydrate: 31g
- Protein: 2g
- Fiber: 1g

208. RubyRed Beet Salad

Adapted from a recipe that I've had for about 30 years, this salad was a big hit when I served it to my future in-laws. -- Toni Talbott, Fairbanks, Alaska

Serving: 12-15 servings. | Prep: 15 m | Cook: 0 m | Ready in: 15 m

Ingredients

- 1 package (3 ounces) cherry gelatin
- 1 package (3 ounces) raspberry gelatin
- 1 package (3 ounces) strawberry gelatin

- 4 cups boiling water
- 1 can (20 ounces) crushed pineapple
- 1 can (15 ounces) diced beets, drained
- DRESSING:
- 1/2 cup mayonnaise
- 1/2 cup sour cream
- 3 tablespoons each chopped celery, green pepper and chives
- Leaf lettuce, optional

Direction

- In a large bowl, combine the gelatins; add boiling water and stir to dissolve. Drain pineapple, reserving the juice; set pineapple aside. Stir juice into gelatin. Refrigerate until slightly thickened. Stir in beets and pineapple. Pour into a 13-in. x 9-in. dish. Refrigerate until firm.
- For dressing, combine the mayonnaise, sour cream, celery, green pepper and chives in a small bowl. Cut gelatin into squares; serve on lettuce-lined salad plates if desired. Dollop with dressing.

Nutrition Information

- Calories: 164 calories
- Total Fat: 7g
- Cholesterol: 8mg
- Sodium: 139mg
- Total Carbohydrate: 23g
- Protein: 2g
- Fiber: 1g

209. Sailboat Salads

These salads are fun to assemble and a terrific way to get kids to eat fruit. It is so cute, kids will sail them right to the dinner table, where their siblings are sure to reward them with happy waves of applause.--Lee Nelson, Waco, Texas

Serving: 4 servings. | Prep: 15 m | Cook: 0 m | Ready in: 15 m

Ingredients

- 1 package (3 ounces) berry blue gelatin
- 1 cup boiling water
- 1 cup cold water
- 1 can (29 ounces) peach halves, drained
- 4 toothpicks
- 2 thick slices process American cheese
- 2 cups torn lettuce

Direction

- Place gelatin in a bowl; add boiling water and stir until gelatin is dissolved. Stir in cold water. Pour gelatin onto four salad plates; refrigerate until firm. For boat, place a peach half, cut side up, in the center of each plate (refrigerate any remaining peaches for another use). Cut cheese slices in half diagonally. For sail, carefully insert a toothpick into the top center of each cheese triangle. Bend cheese slightly; push toothpick through bottom center of cheese. Insert toothpick into edge of peach. Arrange lettuce around plate.

Nutrition Information

- Calories: 264 calories
- Total Fat: 3g
- Cholesterol: 7mg
- Sodium: 190mg
- Total Carbohydrate: 61g
- Protein: 5g
- Fiber: 3g

210. SchoolColors Salad

Now you can be true to your graduate's school--thanks to Torrington, Connecticut resident Andrea Holcomb's clever concoction. You simply make colored gelatins in the school's hues. Andrea notes, "This salad is really easy to put together. In fact, it's an ideal do-ahead dish."--Andrea Holcomb, Torrington, Connecticut

Serving: 12-16 servings. | Prep: 30 m | Cook: 0 m | Ready in: 30 m

Ingredients

- 2 packages (3 ounces each) lime gelatin
- 1 package (3 ounces) lemon gelatin
- 4-1/2 cups boiling water, divided
- 1 envelope unflavored gelatin
- 1/4 cup cold water
- 1 cup heavy whipping cream
- 1/4 cup sugar
- 1 cup sour cream

Direction

- In three separate bowls, dissolve each package of flavored gelatin in 1-1/2 cups boiling water. Pour one bowl of lime gelatin into an oiled 8-cup serving bowl or mold; chill until almost set, about 1 hour. Set other two bowls of gelatin aside at room temperature.
- Soften unflavored gelatin in cold water; let stand 5 minutes. Heat cream in a medium saucepan over medium heat just below boiling. Stir in softened gelatin and sugar until dissolved. Remove from the heat; stir in sour cream until smooth. Carefully spoon half over chilled lime gelatin layer. Chill until almost set, about 30 minutes.
- Carefully spoon lemon gelatin over cream layer. Chill until almost set, about 1 hour.
- Stir remaining cream mixture; carefully spoon over lemon layer. Chill until almost set, about 30 minutes.
- Carefully spoon the second bowl of lime gelatin over cream layer. Chill several hours or overnight. Unmold if a mold was used.

Nutrition Information

- Calories:
- Total Fat: g
- Cholesterol: mg
- Sodium: mg
- Total Carbohydrate: g
- Protein: g
- Fiber: g

211. Seaside Gelatin Salad

This busy beach scene is easy to create when you stir crushed pineapple into berry blue gelatin, chill, then top with graham cracker crumb "sand". Add fun details with simple store-bought items like gummy fish, chocolate seashells, paper umbrellas and more.

Serving: 12-15 servings. | Prep: 15 m | Cook: 0 m | Ready in: 15 m

Ingredients

- 4 packages (3 ounces each) berry blue gelatin
- 3 cups boiling water
- 3 cups cold water
- 1 can (20 ounces) crushed pineapple, drained
- 1-3/4 cups graham cracker crumbs
- 6 tablespoons butter, melted
- 1/4 cup sugar
- Candies for decorating

Direction

- In a large bowl, dissolve gelatin in boiling water. Stir in cold water and pineapple. Pour into a 13-in. x 9-in. dish. Refrigerate until set. In a bowl, combine the cracker crumbs, butter and sugar; cover and refrigerate. Just before serving, sprinkle cracker mixture over half of the gelatin to form a beach. Decorate as desired.

Nutrition Information

- Calories: 138 calories
- Total Fat: 6g
- Cholesterol: 12mg
- Sodium: 119mg

- Total Carbohydrate: 22g
- Protein: 1g
- Fiber: 1g

212. SevenLayer Gelatin Salad

By alternating fruity layers of gelatin in harvest colors with sweetened sour cream, Melody Mellinger of Myerstown, Pennsylvania created one eye-catching treat. "Kids really fall for it," she says with a laugh, "but it's impressive enough to satisfy any adult."

Serving: 12-15 servings. | Prep: 20 m | Cook: 10 m | Ready in: 30 m

Ingredients

- 1 package (3 ounces) cherry gelatin
- 4 cups boiling water, divided
- 2-1/2 cups cold water, divided
- 2 envelopes unflavored gelatin
- 2 cups milk
- 1 cup sugar
- 2 cups (16 ounces) sour cream
- 2 teaspoons vanilla extract
- 1 package (3 ounces) lemon gelatin
- 1 package (3 ounces) orange gelatin
- 1 package (3 ounces) lime gelatin

Direction

- In a bowl, dissolve cherry gelatin in 1 cup boiling water. Add 1/2 cup cold water; stir. Pour into a 13-in. x 9-in. dish coated with cooking spray; refrigerate until set but not firm, about 30 minutes.
- In a small saucepan, sprinkle unflavored gelatin over 1/2 cup cold water. Let stand for 1 minute. Stir in milk and sugar. Cook and stir over medium heat until gelatin and sugar are dissolved.
- Remove from the heat. Whisk in sour cream and vanilla until smooth. Spoon 1-2/3 cups creamy gelatin mixture over the first flavored layer. Chill until set but not firm. Prepare remaining flavored gelatin as directed for

cherry gelatin. Alternately layer flavored gelatins with creamy gelatin layers, allowing each to set before adding next layer. Top with lime gelatin. Refrigerate overnight. Cut into squares.

Nutrition Information

- Calories: 222 calories
- Total Fat: 6g
- Cholesterol: 26mg
- Sodium: 85mg
- Total Carbohydrate: 36g
- Protein: 5g
- Fiber: 0 g

213. Simple Lime Gelatin Salad

Looking for a festive dish to light up the buffet? This pretty green gelatin salad is eye-catching and has a delightful, tangy flavor. --Cyndi Fynaardt, Oskaloosa, Iowa

Serving: 10 servings. | Prep: 20 m | Cook: 0 m | Ready in: 20 m

Ingredients

- 2 packages (3 ounces each) lime gelatin
- 2 cups boiling water
- 1 quart lime sherbet
- 1 carton (8 ounces) frozen whipped topping, thawed

Direction

- In a large bowl, dissolve gelatin in boiling water. Beat in sherbet until melted. Add whipped topping; beat well.
- Pour into an 8-cup ring mold coated with cooking spray. Refrigerate for 4 hours or until set. Unmold onto a serving platter.

Nutrition Information

- Calories: 210 calories
- Total Fat: 5g
- Cholesterol: 0 mg

- Sodium: 66mg
- Total Carbohydrate: 38g
- Protein: 2g
- Fiber: 2g

214. SixLayer Gelatin Salad

This impressive salad does take some time to make, but the preparation itself is actually easy. It's an attractive addition to a buffet table. --Marcia Orlando, Boyertown, Pennsylvania

Serving: 16-20 servings. | Prep: 40 m | Cook: 0 m | Ready in: 40 m

Ingredients

- 2 packages (3 ounces each) lime gelatin
- 4-1/2 cups boiling water, divided
- 4-1/2 cups cold water, divided
- 1 cup heavy whipping cream
- 3 tablespoons confectioners' sugar
- 2 packages (3 ounces each) orange gelatin
- 1 can (8 ounces) crushed pineapple, drained
- 1 package (3 ounces) strawberry gelatin
- 2 medium firm bananas, thinly sliced

Direction

- In a bowl, dissolve one package of lime gelatin in 3/4 cup boiling water; stir in 3/4 cup cold water. Refrigerate until slightly thickened. In a small bowl, beat cream until slightly thickened. Add sugar; beat until soft peaks form. Fold in a third of the whipped cream into the lime gelatin. Spoon into a 4-qt. bowl. Refrigerate until firm. Refrigerate remaining whipped cream.
- In a bowl, dissolve one package of orange gelatin in 3/4 cup boiling water; stir in 3/4 cup cold water. Refrigerate until slightly thickened. Fold in mandarin oranges. Spoon over creamy lime layer. Refrigerate until firm.
- In a bowl, dissolve lemon gelatin in 3/4 cup boiling water; stir in 3/4 cup cold water. Refrigerate until slightly thickened. Fold in a third of the whipped cream. Spoon over orange layer. Refrigerate until firm.
- In a bowl, dissolve remaining package of lime gelatin in 3/4 cup boiling water; stir in 3/4 cup cold water. Refrigerate until slightly thickened. Fold in pineapple. Spoon over creamy lemon layer. Refrigerate until firm.
- In a bowl, dissolve remaining package of orange gelatin in 3/4 cup boiling water; stir in 3/4 cup cold water. Refrigerate until slightly thickened. Fold in remaining whipped cream. Spoon over lime layer. Refrigerate until firm.
- In a bowl, dissolve strawberry gelatin in remaining boiling water; stir in remaining cold water. Refrigerate until slightly thickened. Fold in bananas. Spoon over creamy orange layer. Refrigerate overnight.

Nutrition Information

- Calories: 109 calories
- Total Fat: 4g
- Cholesterol: 16mg
- Sodium: 34mg
- Total Carbohydrate: 17g
- Protein: 2g
- Fiber: 0 g

215. Slimy Red Goop Salad

This frightfully fun salad features cola, which adds to the bright, sparkling taste.

Serving: 8 servings. | Prep: 20 m | Cook: 0 m | Ready in: 20 m

Ingredients

- 1 can (15 ounces) mandarin oranges
- 1/2 cup water
- 2 packages (3 ounces each) cherry gelatin
- 1 can (21 ounces) cherry pie filling
- 3/4 cup cola

Direction

- Drain mandarin oranges, reserving juice; set fruit aside. In a large saucepan, bring mandarin orange juice and water to a boil; remove from the heat. Stir in gelatin until dissolved. Stir in pie filling and cola.
- Pour into a 1-1/2-qt. serving bowl. Refrigerate for 50 minutes or until slightly thickened. Fold in reserved oranges. Refrigerate 3 hours longer or until set.

Nutrition Information

- Calories: 166 calories
- Total Fat: 0 g
- Cholesterol: 0 mg
- Sodium: 42mg
- Total Carbohydrate: 41g
- Protein: 1g
- Fiber: 1g

216. SnowWhite Salad

I love to collect recipes for all kinds of occasions. This sweet gelatin salad is one I often make for Christmas, decorating it with halved red candied cherries for "holly berries" and green candied cherries cut into "leaves".

Serving: 16 servings. | Prep: 25 m | Cook: 0 m | Ready in: 25 m

Ingredients

- 2 envelopes unflavored gelatin
- 1/2 cup cold water
- 1 can (20 ounces) crushed pineapple, undrained
- 1/4 cup sugar
- 2 packages (8 ounces each) cream cheese, softened
- 1 jar (7 ounces) marshmallow creme
- 2 envelopes whipped topping mix (Dream Whip)
- Red and green candied cherries, optional

Direction

- In a small bowl, combine gelatin and water; set aside. In a saucepan, bring pineapple and sugar to a boil. Remove from the heat; stir in gelatin mixture until completely dissolved.
- In a large bowl, beat cream cheese until fluffy. Stir in marshmallow creme and pineapple mixture. Refrigerate for 30 minutes.
- Prepare whipped topping according to package directions; fold into pineapple mixture. Pour into an ungreased 13-in. x 9-in. dish. Cover and refrigerate overnight. Decorate with cherries if desired.

Nutrition Information

- Calories: 141 calories
- Total Fat: 5g
- Cholesterol: 16mg
- Sodium: 54mg
- Total Carbohydrate: 21g
- Protein: 2g
- Fiber: 0 g

217. Snowy Raspberry Gelatin Mold

This mold is always on our holiday table. The raspberry layer makes an eye-catching base for the creamy cream cheese layer. --Lily Julow, Lawrenceville, Georgia

Serving: 8 servings. | Prep: 25 m | Cook: 5 m | Ready in: 30 m

Ingredients

- 1 envelope unflavored gelatin
- 1/2 cup cold water
- 1 cup half-and-half cream
- 1/2 cup sugar
- 1 package (8 ounces) cream cheese, softened
- 1 teaspoon vanilla extract
- 1 package (3 ounces) raspberry gelatin
- 1 cup boiling water
- 1 package (10 ounces) frozen sweetened raspberries, thawed
- Fresh raspberries, optional

Direction

- In a small bowl, sprinkle unflavored gelatin over cold water; let stand for 1 minute. In a small saucepan, combine half-and-half and sugar. Cook and stir just until mixture comes to a simmer. Remove from the heat; stir into gelatin until dissolved.
- In a large bowl, beat cream cheese until smooth. Fold in gelatin mixture. Stir in vanilla. Pour into a 6-cup mold coated with cooking spray. Refrigerate until set but not firm, about 45 minutes.
- In a small bowl, dissolve raspberry gelatin in boiling water. Stir in raspberries until blended. Carefully spoon over cream cheese layer. Cover and refrigerate for at least 4 hours.
- Unmold onto a serving plate; garnish with fresh berries if desired.

Nutrition Information

- Calories: 267 calories
- Total Fat: 13g
- Cholesterol: 46mg
- Sodium: 125mg
- Total Carbohydrate: 33g
- Protein: 5g
- Fiber: 2g

218. Sparkling Gelatin Salad

Fruit really shines though this refreshing gelatin salad.-- Cassie Alexander, Muncie, Indiana

Serving: 6 servings. | Prep: 15 m | Cook: 0 m | Ready in: 15 m

Ingredients

- 2 envelopes unflavored gelatin
- 1-1/2 cups white grape juice, divided
- 1-1/2 cups sweet white wine or additional white grape juice
- 1/4 cup sugar
- 1 can (15 ounces) mandarin oranges, drained

- 1 cup green grapes, halved
- 3/4 cup fresh raspberries

Direction

- In a small saucepan, sprinkle gelatin over 1/2 cup juice; let stand for 1 minute. Heat over low heat, stirring until gelatin is completely dissolved. Stir in the wine, sugar and remaining juice. Cook and stir until sugar is dissolved.
- Pour into a 1-1/2-qt. serving bowl. Refrigerate until set but not firm, about 1 hour. Fold in the oranges, grapes and raspberries. Refrigerate until firm.

Nutrition Information

- Calories: 179 calories
- Total Fat: 0 g
- Cholesterol: 0 mg
- Sodium: 15mg
- Total Carbohydrate: 32g
- Protein: 3g
- Fiber: 2g

219. Sparkling Rhubarb Salad

To sweeten your meal, give subscriber Mary Ellen Beachy's rhubarb salad a try. "It has a very fresh fruity flavor," she remarks from Dundee, Ohio. "Plus, it comes in handy if you find you have a surplus harvest of rhubarb to use up-- like we do each summer!"--Mary Ellen Beach, Dundee, Ohio

Serving: 8-10 servings. | Prep: 15 m | Cook: 0 m | Ready in: 15 m

Ingredients

- 4 cups diced fresh or frozen rhubarb
- 1-1/2 cups water
- 1/2 cup sugar
- 2 packages (3 ounces each) strawberry gelatin
- 1 cup orange juice
- 1 tablespoon grated orange zest
- 2 cups sliced fresh strawberries

Direction

- In a large saucepan, combine the rhubarb, water and sugar. Cook over medium heat until the rhubarb is tender, about 5 minutes. Remove from the heat. Stir in gelatin until dissolved. Add orange juice and zest. Chill for 2 to 2-1/2 hours or until slightly thickened.
- Stir in the strawberries; pour into a 2-qt. bowl. Chill for 2-3 hours or until firm.

Nutrition Information

- Calories:
- Total Fat: g
- Cholesterol: mg
- Sodium: mg
- Total Carbohydrate: g
- Protein: g
- Fiber: g

220. Special Strawberry Salad

This berry-filled salad may take some time to prepare, but one taste and you'll agree it's worth the extra effort. I treat family and friends to this dish on special occasions. --Linda Goulet, Hadley, Massachusetts

Serving: 10-12 servings. | Prep: 20 m | Cook: 0 m | Ready in: 20 m

Ingredients

- 1 envelope unflavored gelatin
- 1/4 cup cold water
- 1 cup half-and-half cream
- 2/3 cup sugar
- 2 cups sour cream
- 1 teaspoon vanilla extract
- 1 package (6 ounces) strawberry gelatin
- 2 cups boiling water
- 1 package (16 ounces) unsweetened frozen strawberries
- 1 can (11 ounces) mandarin oranges

Direction

- Dissolve unflavored gelatin in cold water. In a medium saucepan over low heat, heat cream and sugar until sugar dissolves. Stir in gelatin mixture until dissolved. Remove from the heat; stir in sour cream and vanilla. Pour into a 2-qt. glass bowl; chill until firm. Dissolve strawberry gelatin in boiling water. Drain orange liquid into strawberry gelatin; blend well. Gently stir in strawberries until thawed. Pour over cream layer; arrange oranges on top (allow to settle) and chill until firm.

Nutrition Information

- Calories: 233 calories
- Total Fat: 9g
- Cholesterol: 37mg
- Sodium: 66mg
- Total Carbohydrate: 33g
- Protein: 4g
- Fiber: 1g

221. Spiced Cranberry Gelatin Mold

I love serving this pretty salad to guest. Children also love it so you can also serve it for dessert.--Sherry Conley, Noel Hants County, Nova Scotia

Serving: 10 servings. | Prep: 15 m | Cook: 0 m | Ready in: 15 m

Ingredients

- 2 packages (3 ounces each) cranberry gelatin
- 2 cups boiling water
- 1-1/2 cups chilled cranberry juice
- 1 tablespoon lemon juice
- 3/4 teaspoon ground cinnamon
- 1/4 teaspoon ground cloves
- 1-1/2 cups finely chopped fresh or frozen cranberries, thawed
- 3/4 cup sugar

- 1 medium navel orange, peeled and finely chopped
- 1/2 cup chopped pecans
- Lettuce leaves

Direction

- In a large bowl, dissolve gelatin in boiling water. Let stand for 10 minutes. Stir in the cranberry juice, lemon juice, cinnamon and cloves; refrigerate for 1 hour or until partially set.
- Combine the cranberries, sugar, orange and pecans; fold into gelatin mixture. Pour into a 6-cup ring mold coated with cooking spray. Refrigerate for 4 hours or until set. Unmold onto a lettuce-lined platter.

Nutrition Information

- Calories: 191 calories
- Total Fat: 4g
- Cholesterol: 0 mg
- Sodium: 40mg
- Total Carbohydrate: 38g
- Protein: 2g
- Fiber: 2g

222. Spiced CranberryChutney Gelatin Salad

I combined my mother-in-law's famous cranberry chutney with my raspberry gelatin recipe to come up with this nicely spiced side. It's wonderful served alongside turkey, chicken or beef. --Barbara Estabrook, Rhinelander, Wisconsin

Serving: 12 servings. | Prep: 25 m | Cook: 30 m | Ready in: 55 m

Ingredients

- 1 cup sugar
- 1 cup water
- 2 cups fresh or frozen cranberries
- 1/2 cup golden raisins
- 1/4 cup red wine vinegar
- 1 tablespoon molasses
- 1-1/2 teaspoons Worcestershire sauce
- 1 teaspoon ground ginger
- 1/2 teaspoon curry powder
- 1/4 teaspoon salt
- 1/4 teaspoon ground nutmeg
- 1/4 cup chopped salted roasted almonds
- GELATIN:
- 1 package (6 ounces) raspberry gelatin
- 1-1/2 cups boiling water
- 1/2 cup cold water
- 12 red lettuce leaves
- 3/4 cup sour cream
- 1/4 cup chopped salted roasted almonds

Direction

- In a large saucepan, combine sugar and water. Bring to a boil over medium heat. Reduce heat; simmer, uncovered, for 5 minutes. Stir in cranberries; cook over medium heat until the berries pop, about 15 minutes.
- Stir in the raisins, vinegar, molasses, Worcestershire sauce, ginger, curry, salt and nutmeg. Reduce heat; simmer, uncovered, for 15 minutes, stirring occasionally. Transfer to a large bowl; cool to room temperature. Stir in almonds.
- Meanwhile, for gelatin, in a large bowl, dissolve gelatin in boiling water. Stir in cold water. Add cranberry mixture. Transfer to an 11x7-in. dish coated with cooking spray. Cover and refrigerate for at least 4 hours or until set.
- Serve on lettuce leaves. Top with sour cream and almonds.

Nutrition Information

- Calories: 215 calories
- Total Fat: 6g
- Cholesterol: 10mg
- Sodium: 117mg
- Total Carbohydrate: 39g
- Protein: 3g
- Fiber: 2g

223. Spiced Orange Gelatin Salad

This lovely molded salad looks and tastes festive. Its orange and cinnamon flavor combination will make it a popular side dish for most any entrée.--Jennifer Kauffman Figueroa, Greenville, South Carolina

Serving: 8 servings. | Prep: 15 m | Cook: 0 m | Ready in: 15 m

Ingredients

- 2 packages (3 ounces each) orange gelatin, divided
- 1-3/4 cups boiling water, divided
- 3/4 cup cold water
- 1 cup sweetened applesauce
- 1 cup (8 ounces) sour cream
- 1/4 teaspoon ground cinnamon
- Lettuce leaves and sliced apples, optional

Direction

- In a large bowl, dissolve one package of gelatin in 1 cup boiling water. Stir in cold water. Pour into a 6-cup ring mold coated with cooking spray. Refrigerate until set but not firm, about 1 hour.
- Meanwhile, in a large bowl, dissolve remaining package of gelatin in remaining boiling water. Stir in the applesauce, sour cream and cinnamon. Refrigerate for 1 hour or until thickened. Gently spread over gelatin in mold. Refrigerate until firm.
- Line a serving plate with lettuce leaves if desired; unmold gelatin onto plate. Garnish with apples and additional lettuce if desired.

Nutrition Information

- Calories: 162 calories
- Total Fat: 5g
- Cholesterol: 20mg
- Sodium: 60mg
- Total Carbohydrate: 26g
- Protein: 3g
- Fiber: 0 g

224. Spiced Peach Salad

This refreshing salad is my most requested recipe. A touch of cinnamon makes it taste like fresh peach pie. My father-in-law is an especially big fan of this fruity salad, and I know you'll love it, too. -Karen Hamilton, Ludington, Michigan

Serving: 8-10 servings. | Prep: 25 m | Cook: 0 m | Ready in: 25 m

Ingredients

- 1/2 cup sugar
- 3 tablespoons white vinegar
- 2 cups water
- 1 tablespoon whole cloves
- 4 cinnamon sticks
- 2 packages (3 ounces each) peach or orange gelatin
- 1 can (29 ounces) peach halves

Direction

- In a large saucepan, combine the sugar, vinegar and water. Tie cloves and cinnamon in a cheesecloth bag; place in the saucepan. Bring to a boil. Reduce heat; simmer, uncovered, for 10 minutes.
- Remove from the heat and discard spice bag. Add gelatin; stir until dissolved. Drain peaches, reserving syrup; set peaches aside. Add water to syrup to equal 2 cups. Add to gelatin mixture; stir well.
- Chill until slightly thickened. Thinly slice peaches; add to gelatin. Pour into a 2-qt. glass bowl; chill until firm.

Nutrition Information

- Calories: 161 calories
- Total Fat: 0 g
- Cholesterol: 0 mg
- Sodium: 44mg
- Total Carbohydrate: 41g
- Protein: 2g
- Fiber: 1g

225. Spicy Citrus Gelatin Mold

"This old family recipe is delicious served with ham or turkey," shares Joan Hallford from North Richland Hills, Texas. "The sour cream dressing adds a nice tang and everyone comes back for seconds when I serve it."

Serving: 8 servings. | Prep: 30 m | Cook: 0 m | Ready in: 30 m

Ingredients

- 2 cans (11 ounces each) mandarin oranges
- 1 cinnamon stick (3 inches)
- 8 whole cloves
- 1/8 teaspoon salt
- 1 package (.3 ounce) sugar-free lemon gelatin
- 1 package (.3 ounce) sugar-free orange gelatin
- 1 cup cranberry juice
- 1/4 cup lemon juice
- DRESSING:
- 1 cup (8 ounces) fat-free sour cream
- 1 tablespoon orange juice
- 1 tablespoon honey
- 2 teaspoons grated orange zest
- 1/8 teaspoon salt

Direction

- Drain oranges, reserving juice; set oranges aside. Add enough water to juice to measure 2-1/2 cups; pour into a large saucepan. Add the cinnamon stick, cloves and salt. Bring to a boil. Reduce heat; cover and simmer for 10 minutes. Cool slightly. Strain liquid; discard spices.
- Return liquid to pan and return to a boil. In a large bowl, combine the lemon and orange gelatins; add boiling liquid and stir until dissolved. Stir in cranberry and lemon juices. Cover and refrigerate until syrupy, about 45 minutes. Fold in mandarin oranges. Transfer to a 1-1/2-qt. mold coated with cooking spray. Cover and refrigerate until firm.
- In a small bowl, combine dressing ingredients. Unmold gelatin onto a serving platter; serve with dressing.

Nutrition Information

- Calories: 113 calories
- Total Fat: 0 g
- Cholesterol: 4mg
- Sodium: 154mg
- Total Carbohydrate: 25g
- Protein: 3g
- Fiber: 1g

226. Spinach Salad Ring

I've been serving this salad on special occasions for more than 20 years. It's a new and interesting way to eat spinach.

Serving: 10-12 servings. | Prep: 30 m | Cook: 0 m | Ready in: 30 m

Ingredients

- 2 envelopes unflavored gelatin
- 1 can (10-1/2 ounces) condensed beef broth, undiluted
- 1/4 cup water
- 2 tablespoons lemon juice
- 1/2 teaspoon salt
- 1 cup mayonnaise
- 1 package (10 ounces) frozen chopped spinach, thawed and squeezed dry
- 4 hard-boiled large eggs, chopped
- 1/4 pound sliced bacon, cooked and crumbled
- 1/4 cup thinly sliced green onions
- Cherry tomatoes, optional

Direction

- In a saucepan, sprinkle gelatin over broth; let stand for 5 minutes. Cook over low heat until gelatin is dissolved. Add water, lemon juice and salt; mix well.
- Place mayonnaise in a bowl. Gradually add broth mixture, stirring constantly until smooth. Chill until slightly thickened, about 40 minutes. Fold in spinach, eggs, bacon and onions. Pour into a greased 6-cup mold. Chill until firm.

- When ready to serve, unmold onto a platter; garnish with tomatoes if desired.

Nutrition Information

- Calories: 192 calories
- Total Fat: 18g
- Cholesterol: 80mg
- Sodium: 480mg
- Total Carbohydrate: 2g
- Protein: 5g
- Fiber: 1g

227. Spring Rhubarb Salad

In our part of Iowa, we know spring is coming when we see the first rhubarb peeking out of the ground. We enjoy it so much that it's hard to wait for the stalks to grow large enough to be picked! I've collected lots of recipes for rhubarb, but this is one of my family's favorites.

Serving: 8-10 servings. | Prep: 10 m | Cook: 10 m | Ready in: 20 m

Ingredients

- 4 cups diced fresh rhubarb
- 1-1/2 cups water
- 1/2 cup sugar
- 1 package (6 ounces) strawberry gelatin
- 1 cup orange juice
- 1 teaspoon grated orange zest
- 1 cup sliced fresh strawberries

Direction

- Combine rhubarb, water and sugar in saucepan. Cook and stir over medium heat until rhubarb is tender. Remove from heat; add gelatin and stir until dissolved. Add orange juice and zest. Chill until syrupy. Add strawberries. Pour into 6-cup mold; chill until set.

Nutrition Information

- Calories: 127 calories
- Total Fat: 0 g
- Cholesterol: 0 mg

- Sodium: 41mg
- Total Carbohydrate: 31g
- Protein: 2g
- Fiber: 1g

228. Springtime Luncheon Salad

I discovered this recipe when I was looking for meals to serve on warm days. Chicken salad nestled in a molden gelatin ring makes this a perfect light luncheon. Even my son likes it...and he's the pickiest eater on the planet! -Julie Dillion, Boise, Idaho

Serving: 8-10 servings. | Prep: 30 m | Cook: 0 m | Ready in: 30 m

Ingredients

- 2 envelopes unflavored gelatin
- 2-1/2 cups orange juice, divided
- 2 cups sugar
- Dash salt
- 4 large egg yolks, lightly beaten
- 3 medium navel oranges, peeled and sectioned
- 3 tablespoons lemon juice
- 1 teaspoon grated orange zest
- 1 teaspoon grated lemon zest
- 2 cups heavy whipping cream, whipped
- CHICKEN SALAD:
- 6 cups cubed cooked chicken
- 1 cup chopped celery
- 1 cup mayonnaise
- 1/8 teaspoon white vinegar
- Salt and pepper to taste
- 1/2 cup heavy whipping cream whipped
- 1/2 cup sliced almonds, toasted
- Orange peel strips and fresh thyme, optional

Direction

- In a large saucepan, sprinkle gelatin over 1 cup orange juice; let stand for 1 minute. Stir in sugar and salt. Cook and stir over low heat until gelatin and sugar are completely dissolved. Remove from the heat. Stir a small amount of hot mixture into egg yolks; return all to the pan, stirring constantly. Bring to a gentle boil; cook and stir for 2 minutes longer. Remove from the heat.

- Stir in the orange sections, lemon juice, grated zest and remaining orange juice. Cool.
- Fold in whipped cream. Pour into a 9-cup ring mold coated with cooking spray. Chill until set.
- In a large bowl, combine chicken and celery. In a small bowl, combine mayonnaise, vinegar, salt and pepper; fold in whipped cream. Fold into chicken mixture.
- Unmold gelatin onto a serving platter. Fill center with chicken salad. Sprinkle with almonds. Serve with orange peel and thyme if desired.

Nutrition Information

- Calories: 786 calories
- Total Fat: 50g
- Cholesterol: 249mg
- Sodium: 246mg
- Total Carbohydrate: 55g
- Protein: 30g
- Fiber: 2g

---

229. Strawberry Apple Salad

Although I live in the city now, I was born and raised in the country in Wayne County, Ohio. Our county and the neighboring one, Holmes, had a high Amish population, and it is from one of my Amish friends that I received this recipe. It is traditionally served at weddings in some Amish circles.

Serving: 15 servings. | Prep: 20 m | Cook: 10 m | Ready in: 30 m

Ingredients

- 1 can (20 ounces) crushed pineapple
- 2 packages (3 ounces each) strawberry gelatin
- 2 cups boiling water
- 2 cups diced peeled apples
- 1/2 cup sugar

- 2 tablespoons all-purpose flour
- 1 large egg, beaten
- 2 tablespoons butter
- 4 ounces cream cheese, softened
- 1 envelope whipped topping mix (Dream Whip)

Direction

- Drain pineapple, reserving juice; set aside 1/2 cup. To remaining juice, add enough cold water to measure 2 cups.
- In a bowl, dissolve gelatin in boiling water; stir in the juice/water mixture. Add pineapple and apples. Pour into a 13x9-in. dish coated with cooking spray; cover and chill until firm.
- In a small saucepan, combine sugar and flour. Stir in reserved pineapple juice until smooth. Cook and stir over medium-high heat until thickened and bubbly. Reduce heat to low; cook and stir for 2 minutes longer. Remove from the heat. Stir a small amount (or give the amount) of hot filling into egg; return all to the pan, stirring constantly. Bring to a gentle boil; cook and stir for 2 minutes. Remove from the heat; gently stir in cream cheese until smooth. Cool.
- Prepare whipped topping mix according to package directions. Fold whipped topping into cream cheese mixture. Spread over gelatin. Cover and chill until topping is set, about 3 hours.

Nutrition Information

- Calories: 161 calories
- Total Fat: 5g
- Cholesterol: 27mg
- Sodium: 68mg
- Total Carbohydrate: 28g
- Protein: 2g
- Fiber: 1g

230. Strawberry Bavarian Salad

"As a child, I asked my mother to make this colorful gelatin for birthdays," recalls Lorna Northcutt of Gladstone, Oregon. "Now I fix it for my husband and son. You can leave out the marshmallows if you prefer," she adds.

Serving: 6 servings. | Prep: 15 m | Cook: 0 m | Ready in: 15 m

Ingredients

- 1 package (3 ounces) strawberry gelatin
- 1 cup boiling water
- 2 packages (10 ounces each) frozen sweetened sliced strawberries
- 1 cup miniature marshmallows
- 1/2 cup heavy whipping cream, whipped

Direction

- In a large bowl, dissolve gelatin in water. Stir in the strawberries; fold in marshmallows and whipped cream. Transfer to a 5-cup serving bowl. Cover and refrigerate overnight.

Nutrition Information

- Calories: 185 calories
- Total Fat: 4g
- Cholesterol: 14mg
- Sodium: 42mg
- Total Carbohydrate: 39g
- Protein: 2g
- Fiber: 1g

231. Strawberry Gelatin Salad

Even though it's low-fat, this salad is always a hit when served at church dinners and family reunions. Strawberries, bananas and pineapple give this dish its delightful natural sweetness.--Ruth Barton, Millsap, Texas

Serving: 8 servings. | Prep: 10 m | Cook: 0 m | Ready in: 10 m

Ingredients

- 2 cups frozen unsweetened strawberries
- 2 medium ripe bananas
- Sugar substitute equivalent to 2 tablespoons sugar
- 1 package (.6 ounce) sugar-free strawberry gelatin
- 2 cups boiling water
- 1 can (8 ounces) unsweetened crushed pineapple, undrained
- 1 cup (8 ounces) reduced-fat plain yogurt

Direction

- Mash strawberries, bananas and sugar substitute; set aside. Dissolve gelatin in boiling water. Stir in strawberry mixture and pineapple.
- Pour half into an 8-in. square dish coated with cooking spray. Chill until firm. Combine yogurt and the remaining gelatin mixture; spoon over the first layer. Chill until firm, about 3 hours.

Nutrition Information

- Calories: 86 calories
- Total Fat: 1g
- Cholesterol: 2mg
- Sodium: 76mg
- Total Carbohydrate: 18g
- Protein: 3g
- Fiber: 0 g

232. Strawberry Pear Gelatin

Mother always had a way of making every dish she served just a little more special. A good example is this fluffy salad. It's both fruity and refreshing. -Linda McGinty, Parma, Ohio

Serving: 12-16 servings. | Prep: 15 m | Cook: 0 m | Ready in: 15 m

Ingredients

- 1 can (29 ounces) pears
- 1 package (6 ounces) strawberry gelatin
- 1 package (8 ounces) cream cheese, cubed
- 1 carton (8 ounces) frozen whipped topping, thawed
- Mandarin oranges, optional

Direction

- Drain pears, reserving juice. Chop pears and set aside. Add water to the juice to measure 3 cups. Place in a saucepan; bring to a boil. Add gelatin and stir until dissolved. Whisk in cream cheese until smooth. Refrigerate until slightly thickened. Whisk in whipped topping until smooth. Add chopped pears.
- Transfer to a 13-in. x 9-in. dish. Cover and refrigerate until firm. Cut into squares. Garnish with mandarin oranges if desired.

Nutrition Information

- Calories: 160 calories
- Total Fat: 7g
- Cholesterol: 16mg
- Sodium: 70mg
- Total Carbohydrate: 21g
- Protein: 2g
- Fiber: 0 g

---

233. StrawberryRhubarb Gelatin

The rosy color and tangy flavor of this favorite salad comes through with every refreshing bite. It's a quick, simple salad and an excellent addition to any meal. Our family and friends look forward to this dish when joining us for dinner on the farm. -Kathy Flowers, Burkesville, Kentucky

Serving: 6 servings. | Prep: 20 m | Cook: 0 m | Ready in: 20 m

Ingredients

- 1 cup chopped fresh or frozen rhubarb
- 3/4 cup water
- 1 package (3 ounces) strawberry gelatin
- 1/3 cup sugar
- 1 tablespoon strawberry jam or strawberry spreadable fruit
- 1 cup unsweetened pineapple juice
- 1 medium tart apple, diced
- 1/2 cup chopped walnuts, optional
- Lettuce leaves and mayonnaise, optional

Direction

- In a saucepan over medium heat, bring rhubarb and water to a boil. Reduce heat; cover and simmer for 8-10 minutes or until rhubarb is tender. Remove from the heat. Add the gelatin powder, sugar and jam; stir until gelatin is dissolved. Add pineapple juice. Chill until partially set.
- Stir in apple and nuts if desired. Pour into six 1/2-cup molds or a 1-qt. bowl coated with cooking spray. Chill until set. Unmold onto lettuce leaves if desired and top with a dollop of mayonnaise.

Nutrition Information

- Calories: 96 calories
- Total Fat: 0 g
- Cholesterol: 0 mg
- Sodium: 33mg
- Total Carbohydrate: 24g
- Protein: 1g
- Fiber: 0 g

---

234. SugarFree Cranberry Gelatin Salad

"We don't miss the sugar in this cool, tart and tangy gelatin salad," writes Janet Davis of Atkinson, Nebraska. "It's my family's favorite, especially at the holidays because of its festive color. Walnuts and celery adds a delightful crunch."

Serving: 12 servings. | Prep: 20 m | Cook: 0 m | Ready in: 20 m

Ingredients

- 1 package (12 ounces) fresh or frozen cranberries, thawed
- 1 can (12 ounces) frozen apple juice concentrate, thawed
- 2 packages (.3 ounce each) sugar-free raspberry gelatin
- 1 can (8 ounces) crushed pineapple, undrained
- 1 cup chopped celery

- 1 medium navel orange, peeled, sectioned and chopped
- 1/2 cup chopped walnuts

Direction

- In a 3-qt. microwave-safe dish, combine cranberries and apple juice concentrate; cover with waxed paper. Microwave on high for 6 to, 7-1/2 minutes or until most of the berries have popped. Immediately stir in gelatin powder until dissolved. Cool for 10-15 minutes. Add remaining ingredients; mix well. Pour into a 2-qt. ring mold coated with cooking spray. Refrigerate until firm, about 3 hours. Unmold onto a serving plate just before serving.

Nutrition Information

- Calories: 115 calories
- Total Fat: 3g
- Cholesterol: 0 mg
- Sodium: 49mg
- Total Carbohydrate: 20g
- Protein: 2g
- Fiber: 2g

235. Summertime Strawberry Gelatin Salad

Meet the Cook: For years, this salad has been a "must" at family dinners and special occasions. It's as pretty as it is good, so it's nice for serving at holiday feasts besides. My husband and I have three children, all grown, and a granddaughter. -Janet England, Chillicothe, Missouri

Serving: 12-16 servings. | Prep: 30 m | Cook: 0 m | Ready in: 30 m

Ingredients

- 1 package (3 ounces) strawberry gelatin
- 1 cup boiling water
- 1 cup cold water
- MIDDLE LAYER:
- 1 envelope unflavored gelatin

- 1/2 cup cold water
- 1 cup half-and-half cream
- 1 package (8 ounces) cream cheese, softened
- 1 cup sugar
- 1/2 teaspoon vanilla extract
- TOP LAYER:
- 1 package (6 ounces) strawberry gelatin
- 1 cup boiling water
- 1 cup cold water
- 3 to 4 cups sliced fresh strawberries

Direction

- In a bowl, dissolve strawberry gelatin in boiling water; stir in cold water. Pour into a 13-in. x 9-in. dish coated with cooking spray; refrigerate until set.
- Meanwhile, in a small bowl, sprinkle unflavored gelatin over cold water; let stand for 1 minute. In a saucepan over medium heat, heat cream (do not boil). Add softened gelatin; stir until gelatin is dissolved. Cool to room temperature.
- In a bowl, beat cream cheese, sugar and vanilla until smooth. Gradually add the unflavored gelatin mixture; mix well. Carefully pour over the bottom layer. Refrigerate until set, about 1 hour.
- For top layer, dissolve strawberry gelatin in boiling water; stir in cold water. Cool to room temperature. Stir in strawberries; carefully spoon over middle layer. Refrigerate overnight.

Nutrition Information

- Calories: 187 calories
- Total Fat: 7g
- Cholesterol: 23mg
- Sodium: 87mg
- Total Carbohydrate: 29g
- Protein: 4g
- Fiber: 1g

236. Sunshine Gelatin Mold

"I serve this cool, creamy gelatin on a bed of lettuce and it's always a big hit." A great way to satisfy your sweet tooth!
Marge Nicol, Shannon, Illinois

Serving: 12 servings. | Prep: 15 m | Cook: 0 m | Ready in: 15 m

Ingredients

- 2 packages (3 ounces each) lemon gelatin
- 1 cup boiling water
- 1 quart vanilla ice cream, softened
- 1 can (11 ounces) mandarin oranges, drained
- 1 can (8 ounces) unsweetened crushed pineapple, drained

Direction

- In a large bowl, dissolve gelatin in boiling water. Whisk in ice cream until melted. Stir in oranges and pineapple. Pour into a 6-cup ring mold coated with cooking spray. Refrigerate for 2 hours or until firm. Unmold onto a serving platter.

Nutrition Information

- Calories: 167 calories
- Total Fat: 5g
- Cholesterol: 19mg
- Sodium: 69mg
- Total Carbohydrate: 30g
- Protein: 3g
- Fiber: 0 g

237. Sunshine Gelatin Salad

In Hatley, Wisconsin, Sharon Kriesel offers this festive gelatin salad with a delightful creamy topping and plenty of fruit and marshmallows.

Serving: 12 servings. | Prep: 30 m | Cook: 0 m | Ready in: 30 m

Ingredients

- 1 package (.3 ounce) sugar-free lemon gelatin
- 1 package (.3 ounce) sugar-free orange gelatin
- 2 cups boiling water
- 1-1/2 cups cold water
- 1 can (20 ounces) unsweetened crushed pineapple
- 3 medium firm bananas, chopped
- 1/3 cup miniature marshmallows
- Sugar substitute equivalent to 1/4 cup sugar
- 2 tablespoons all-purpose flour
- 1 egg, lightly beaten
- 2 tablespoons butter, cubed
- 2-1/2 cups whipped topping

Direction

- In a large bowl, dissolve lemon and orange gelatin in boiling water. Stir in cold water. Cover and refrigerate until partially set, about 1-1/2 hours.
- Drain pineapple, reserving juice. Add enough water to juice to measure 1 cup.
- Fold the bananas, marshmallows and pineapple into gelatin mixture. Transfer to a 13-in. x 9-in. dish. Cover and refrigerate until firm.
- In a small saucepan, combine sugar substitute and flour. Gradually stir in pineapple juice mixture. Cook and stir over medium-high heat until thickened and bubbly. Reduce heat; cook and stir 2 minutes longer. Remove from the heat.
- Stir a small amount of hot filling into egg; return all to the pan, stirring constantly. Bring to a gentle boil; cook and stir for 2 minutes. Remove from the heat; stir in butter until melted.
- Cool to room temperature without stirring. Fold in whipped topping. Spread over gelatin. Cover and refrigerate for at least 1 hour before cutting.

Nutrition Information

- Calories: 109 calories
- Total Fat: 4g
- Cholesterol: 18mg
- Sodium: 49mg
- Total Carbohydrate: 16g

- Protein: 2g
- Fiber: 1g

238. Sunshine State Salad

My husband and I retired from central Illinois to Florida. Several times, a friend gave us grapefruit from his backyard tree. One day I was going to make a lemon pineapple gelatin salad and discovered I didn't have pineapple. So, I cut up a fresh grapefruit and used it in the salad. It was good, and I tried adding other fruits until I came up with this recipe. --Doris Wendling, Palm Harbor, Florida

Serving: 8 servings. | Prep: 15 m | Cook: 0 m | Ready in: 15 m

Ingredients

- 1 package (3 ounces) lemon gelatin
- 1 cup boiling water
- 1 can (8 ounces) pineapple chunks, undrained
- 1 large grapefruit, peeled, sectioned and diced
- 1 medium apple, peeled and chopped
- 1/4 cup chopped pecans

Direction

- In a bowl, dissolve gelatin in boiling water. Drain pineapple, reserving juice; set pineapple aside. Add cold water to juice to measure 1 cup; stir into gelatin mixture. Chill until partially set. Stir in grapefruit, apple, pecans and pineapple; pour into a 1-1/2-qt. bowl. Chill until firm.

Nutrition Information

- Calories: 65 calories
- Total Fat: 3g
- Cholesterol: 0 mg
- Sodium: 24mg
- Total Carbohydrate: 10g
- Protein: 1g
- Fiber: 0 g

239. Sweetheart Jello Salad

My cousin served this tasty salad to my family at a memorable Sunday dinner many years ago. I've added this special dish to my menu for Valentine's Day, but I prepare it for other holidays as well. It's so colorful that it adds a festive touch to your table.

Serving: 12-16 servings. | Prep: 20 m | Cook: 0 m | Ready in: 20 m

Ingredients

- 2 envelopes unflavored gelatin
- 1/4 cup cold water
- 1/2 cup sugar
- 1 can (20 ounces) crushed pineapple, undrained
- 2 tablespoons lemon juice
- 1/4 cup maraschino cherry juice
- 6 ounces cream cheese, softened
- 12 maraschino cherries, quartered
- 2 to 3 drops red food coloring, optional
- 1 carton (12 ounces) frozen whipped topping, thawed
- Lettuce leaves, optional

Direction

- Soften gelatin in cold water. Meanwhile, in a saucepan, bring sugar and pineapple with juice to a boil, stirring until the sugar dissolves. Remove from the heat. Add gelatin and stir until dissolved. Add lemon and cherry juices. Cool to lukewarm. Whisk in cream cheese until thoroughly combined. Stir in the cherries and food coloring if desired. Chill until slightly thickened. Fold in whipped topping. Pour into an oiled 13x9-in. pan or 8-1/2-cup mold; chill until firm. Serve the mold or individual squares on lettuce-lined plates if desired.

Nutrition Information

- Calories:
- Total Fat: g
- Cholesterol: mg
- Sodium: mg
- Total Carbohydrate: g

- Protein: g
- Fiber: g

240. Tangy Cucumber Gelatin

A friend shared this recipe with me years ago. She had a vegetable garden and always had a good yield of cucumbers. This pleasant, comforting salad is the right amount for one or two. The cucumber and green onions give a nice texture contrast and refreshing crunch. - Bernadeane McWilliam, Decatur, Illinois

Serving: 2 servings. | Prep: 10 m | Cook: 0 m | Ready in: 10 m

Ingredients

- 1 package (3 ounces) lemon gelatin
- 1/2 cup boiling water
- 1 medium cucumber, peeled and diced
- 4 green onions, chopped
- 1 cup (8 ounces) 4% cottage cheese
- 1/2 cup mayonnaise

Direction

- In a bowl, dissolve gelatin in boiling water. Add the cucumber and onions. Stir in cottage cheese and mayonnaise until blended. Pour into two 1-1/2-cup molds coated with cooking spray. Refrigerate overnight or until set. Unmold just before serving.

Nutrition Information

- Calories: 707 calories
- Total Fat: 49g
- Cholesterol: 45mg
- Sodium: 802mg
- Total Carbohydrate: 48g
- Protein: 19g
- Fiber: 2g

241. Tangy Lemon Gelatin

For years, I didn't know the secret ingredient in my mother's jello which made it so tangy. I finally found it after thumbing through her personal cookbook: Horseradish!--Paula Pelis Marchesi, New York, New York

Serving: 8-10 servings. | Prep: 15 m | Cook: 0 m | Ready in: 15 m

Ingredients

- 1 package (6 ounces) orange gelatin or lemon gelatin
- 2 cups boiling water
- 3/4 cup thawed lemonade concentrate
- 1 to 3 tablespoons prepared horseradish
- 1 carton (8 ounces) frozen whipped topping, thawed
- 2 to 3 tablespoons orange marmalade

Direction

- In a large bowl, dissolve gelatin in boiling water. Stir in lemonade concentrate and horseradish. Cover and refrigerate until partially set, about 1 hour. Stir in whipped topping and marmalade. Coat a 2-qt. ring mold with cooking spray; add gelatin mixture. Chill for at least 4 hours or until firm. Just before serving, invert onto a serving platter.

Nutrition Information

- Calories: 175 calories
- Total Fat: 4g
- Cholesterol: 0 mg
- Sodium: 47mg
- Total Carbohydrate: 33g
- Protein: 2g
- Fiber: 0 g

242. Tart Cherry Salad

This recipe has been in my family for years; we especially use it during the holiday season. It's pleasantly tart and a perfect complement to any meal.

Serving: 16-18 servings. | Prep: 15 m | Cook: 0 m | Ready in: 15 m

Ingredients

- 2 cans (16 ounces each) tart red cherries
- 2 cans (8 ounces each) crushed pineapple
- 1 cup sugar
- 2 packages (6 ounces each) cherry gelatin
- 3 cups ginger ale
- 3/4 cup sweetened shredded coconut
- 1 cup chopped nuts, optional

Direction

- Drain cherries and pineapple, reserving juices. Set fruit aside. Add enough water to combined juices to make 3-1/4 cups; pour into a saucepan. Add sugar; bring to a boil. Remove from the heat; stir in gelatin until dissolved. Add cherries, pineapple and ginger ale. Chill until partially set. Stir in coconut and nuts if desired. Pour into an oiled 3-qt. mold or 13-in. x 9-in. pan. Chill until firm, about 3 hours.

Nutrition Information

- Calories: 137 calories
- Total Fat: 1g
- Cholesterol: 0 mg
- Sodium: 36mg
- Total Carbohydrate: 31g
- Protein: 1g
- Fiber: 0 g

243. Thanksgiving Cranberry Gelatin

This salad has graced my mother's Thanksgiving table for as long as I can remember. --Tiffany Anderson-Taylor, Gulfport, Florida

Serving: 16-20 servings. | Prep: 30 m | Cook: 0 m | Ready in: 30 m

Ingredients

- 1 package (6 ounces) cherry gelatin
- 1/3 to 1/2 cup sugar
- 2 cups boiling cranberry juice
- 1-1/2 cups ice cubes
- 2 celery ribs, finely chopped
- 1 medium pear, peeled and finely chopped
- 1 cup chopped fresh or frozen cranberries
- 3/4 cup ground walnuts, divided
- 1 package (3 ounces) lemon gelatin
- 1 cup boiling water
- 1 cup mayonnaise
- 1 carton (8 ounces) frozen whipped topping, thawed, divided

Direction

- In a large bowl, dissolve cherry gelatin and sugar in boiling cranberry juice. Add the ice cubes; stir until dissolved. Refrigerate until thickened, about 45 minutes.
- Fold in the celery, pear, cranberries and 1/2 cup walnuts. Transfer to a 13-in. x 9-in. dish coated with cooking spray. Refrigerate until firm, about 50 minutes.
- Meanwhile, in another bowl, dissolve lemon gelatin in water. Refrigerate until slightly thickened, about 35 minutes. Whisk in 1/4 cup mayonnaise; fold in the remaining mayonnaise. Fold in half of the whipped topping. Carefully spoon over cherry layer. Refrigerate until firm, about 45 minutes.
- Spread with remaining whipped topping. Sprinkle with remaining walnuts. Refrigerate for at least 3 hours. Cut into squares.

Nutrition Information

- Calories: 210 calories

- Total Fat: 13g
- Cholesterol: 4mg
- Sodium: 93mg
- Total Carbohydrate: 22g
- Protein: 2g
- Fiber: 1g

244. ThreeLayer Fruit Salad

Joyce Siewert of Greendale, Wisconsin layers bananas, pears and apricots in a loaf pan, then covers them with lime gelatin. Rather than spooning out the servings, she slices the salad to showcase the pretty layers. "Sometimes I substitute canned peaches of fruit cocktail for the other canned fruits in the recipe," she says.

Serving: 8 servings. | Prep: 15 m | Cook: 0 m | Ready in: 15 m

Ingredients

- 1 can (15 ounces) pear halves in extra-light syrup
- 2 cans (8-1/4 ounces each) reduced-sugar apricot halves
- 2 medium firm bananas, cut into 1/2-inch slices
- 2 packages (.3 ounce each) sugar-free lime gelatin
- 2 cups boiling water

Direction

- Drain pears and apricots, reserving 1-1/2 cups syrup. In a 9x5-in. loaf pan coated with cooking spray, layer the pears, apricots and bananas. In a large bowl, dissolve gelatin in boiling water. Stir in reserved syrup. Pour gelatin mixture over bananas. Cover and refrigerate until firm. Unmold and slice gelatin.

Nutrition Information

- Calories: 76 calories
- Total Fat: 0 g
- Cholesterol: 0 mg
- Sodium: 62mg
- Total Carbohydrate: 17g

- Protein: 2g
- Fiber: 2g

245. ThreeLayer Gelatin Salad

My love of cooking started in high school. Now I get to try out recipes at church, where my husband is the pastor. My mother-in-law gave me the recipe for this pretty layered salad.

Serving: 12-16 servings. | Prep: 10 m | Cook: 20 m | Ready in: 30 m

Ingredients

- 1 package (3 ounces) raspberry gelatin
- 1 cup boiling water
- 1 package (10 ounces) frozen sweetened raspberries
- ORANGE LAYER:
- 1 can (11 ounces) mandarin oranges
- 1 package (3 ounces) orange gelatin
- 1 cup boiling water
- 1 package (8 ounces) cream cheese, softened
- LIME LAYER:
- 1 package (3 ounces) lime gelatin
- 1 cup boiling water
- 1 can (8-1/2 ounces) crushed pineapple

Direction

- In a large bowl, dissolve gelatin in boiling water. Stir in raspberries until thawed. Pour in a greased 8-in. square dish; refrigerate until set.
- Drain oranges, reserving juice. In small bowl, dissolve orange gelatin in boiling water. In a large bowl, beat cream cheese and reserved juice until smooth. Add gelatin mixture and mix well. Fold in oranges. Pour over raspberry layer; refrigerate until set.
- In a large bowl, dissolve lime gelatin in boiling water. Stir in pineapple; cool for 10 minutes. Carefully spoon over orange layer. Refrigerate until set.

Nutrition Information

- Calories: 149 calories

- Total Fat: 5g
- Cholesterol: 16mg
- Sodium: 80mg
- Total Carbohydrate: 25g
- Protein: 3g
- Fiber: 1g

---

246. ThreeRing Mold

A dear friend shared this recipe with me some 30 years ago. My family never seems to tire of seeing this salad on the table.

Serving: 16-18 servings. | Prep: 30 m | Cook: 0 m | Ready in: 30 m

Ingredients

- FIRST LAYER:
- 2 cans (29 ounces each) pear halves
- 1 package (3 ounces) cherry gelatin
- 3/4 cup boiling water
- SECOND LAYER:
- 1 package (8 ounces) cream cheese, softened
- 1 package (3 ounces) lemon gelatin
- 3/4 cup boiling water
- 3/4 cup cold water
- 1 cup heavy whipping cream, whipped
- THIRD LAYER:
- 1 can (20 ounces) crushed pineapple
- 1 package (3 ounces) lime gelatin
- 3/4 cup boiling water

Direction

- Drain pears, reserving 3/4 cup juice. Arrange pears in a 4-qt. glass bowl or trifle dish. Dissolve cherry gelatin in boiling water; add reserved juice. Pour over pears. Chill until firm.
- For second layer, beat cream cheese in a bowl until smooth and creamy. Dissolve lemon gelatin in boiling water; gradually add to cream cheese. Beat until smooth. Stir in cold water. Add cream and blend until smooth. Pour over first layer. Chill until firm.
- For third layer, drain pineapple, reserving 3/4 cup juice. Dissolve lime gelatin in boiling

water; add pineapple and reserved juice. Pour over second layer. Chill until firm.

Nutrition Information

- Calories: 194 calories
- Total Fat: 9g
- Cholesterol: 32mg
- Sodium: 77mg
- Total Carbohydrate: 27g
- Protein: 3g
- Fiber: 1g

---

247. Triple Cranberry Salad Mold

Whats a holiday meal without at least one jolly gelatin salad chock-full of fruit and nuts? My mother made this one for every holiday, and now my husband says he can't imagine Christmas without it! -Kristi Jo Chiles Portsmouth, Rhode Island

Serving: 8-10 servings. | Prep: 20 m | Cook: 0 m | Ready in: 20 m

Ingredients

- 2 packages (3 ounces each) cranberry gelatin
- 3 cups boiling water
- 1 cup cranberry juice
- 2 packages (3 ounces each) cream cheese, softened
- 1 carton (8 ounces) frozen whipped topping, thawed
- 1 cup chopped walnuts
- 1 cup chopped celery
- 1 cup chopped fresh or frozen cranberries

Direction

- In a large bowl, dissolve the gelatin in boiling water; stir in cranberry juice. Refrigerate until slightly thickened. In a small bowl, beat cream cheese until smooth. Add the whipped topping until blended. Fold into the gelatin mixture. Fold in walnuts, celery and cranberries.

- Pour into a 3-qt. ring mold coated with cooking spray. Refrigerate until set. Unmold onto a serving plate.

Nutrition Information

- Calories: 218 calories
- Total Fat: 14g
- Cholesterol: 9mg
- Sodium: 56mg
- Total Carbohydrate: 19g
- Protein: 5g
- Fiber: 1g

248. Waldorf Orange Cinnamon Holiday Mold

My family prefers this to traditional cranberry gelatin molds. The cinnamon zing really complements ham and turkey. --Nancy Heishman, Las Vegas, Nevada

Serving: 12 servings (1/2 cup each). | Prep: 30 m | Cook: 8 m | Ready in: 38 m

Ingredients

- 2 packages (3 ounces each) cherry gelatin
- 1/2 cup Red Hots
- 1/3 cup sugar
- 1-1/2 cups water
- 1-3/4 cups orange juice
- 1/3 cup sour cream
- 1-1/2 cups orange sections, chopped
- 1 medium apple, peeled and finely chopped
- 1/2 cup chopped pecans

Direction

- Place gelatin in a large bowl. In a small saucepan, combine Red Hots, sugar and water. Cook and stir until candies are dissolved and mixture comes to a boil. Stir into gelatin. Stir in orange juice and sour cream. Refrigerate 30-45 minutes or until thickened. Stir in oranges, apple and pecans. Pour into a 6-cup ring mold

coated with cooking spray. Refrigerate 4 hours or until firm. Unmold onto a platter.

Nutrition Information

- Calories:
- Total Fat: g
- Cholesterol: mg
- Sodium: mg
- Total Carbohydrate: g
- Protein: g
- Fiber: g

249. Waldorf Salad Mold

When I was growing up, my mother would make Waldorf salad during the holiday season using Red Delicious apples. This version is a nice time-saver because you can prepare it ahead of time without the worry of the apples browning.

Serving: 12 servings. | Prep: 25 m | Cook: 0 m | Ready in: 25 m

Ingredients

- 2 packages (3 ounces each) strawberry gelatin
- 2 cups boiling water
- 1-1/2 cups cold water
- 2 medium apples, diced
- 1/2 cup chopped celery
- 1/4 cup chopped walnuts
- LEMON YOGURT DRESSING:
- 3/4 cup (6 ounces) lemon yogurt
- 1-1/2 teaspoons brown sugar
- 1/8 teaspoon salt
- Dash to 1/8 teaspoon ground cinnamon

Direction

- In a large bowl, dissolve gelatin in boiling water. Stir in cold water. Cover and refrigerate until partially set, about 1-1/2 hours. Fold in the apples, celery and walnuts. Pour into a 6-cup ring mold coated with cooking spray. Cover and refrigerate for 4 hours or until set.
- For dressing, combine the yogurt, brown sugar, salt and cinnamon; chill until serving.

To serve, unmold salad onto a platter. Serve with dressing.

Nutrition Information

- Calories: 103 calories
- Total Fat: 2g
- Cholesterol: 2mg
- Sodium: 74mg
- Total Carbohydrate: 19g
- Protein: 3g
- Fiber: 1g

---

250. Whipped Cream Gelatin Mosaic

Small pieces of gelatin give this old-fashioned salad a mosaic look. I like the fact that I don't need a special mold to make it. Serve this as a salad or dessert.--Suzy Horvath, Sheridan, Oregon

Serving: 10 servings. | Prep: 50 m | Cook: 0 m | Ready in: 50 m

Ingredients

- 1 package (3 ounces) cherry gelatin
- 3-3/4 cups boiling water, divided
- 1-1/2 cups cold water, divided
- 1 package (3 ounces) lime gelatin
- 1 package (3 ounces) orange gelatin
- 1 package (3 ounces) lemon gelatin
- 1/4 cup sugar
- 1/2 cup lemonade
- 1-3/4 cups whipped topping
- Additional whipped topping, optional

Direction

- In a small bowl, dissolve cherry gelatin in 1 cup boiling water; stir in 1/2 cup cold water. Pour into an 8-in. square dish coated with cooking spray. Refrigerate until set.
- Repeat with lime and orange gelatin, using separate 8-in. square dishes for each.
- In a large bowl, dissolve lemon gelatin and sugar in remaining boiling water; stir in lemonade. Cover and refrigerate until slightly thickened. Fold in whipped topping.
- Cut the cherry, lime and orange gelatin into 1/2-in. cubes. Fold into lemon gelatin mixture. Spoon into individual serving dishes. Cover and refrigerate for at least 2 hours. Garnish with additional whipped topping if desired.

Nutrition Information

- Calories: 184 calories
- Total Fat: 2g
- Cholesterol: 0 mg
- Sodium: 78mg
- Total Carbohydrate: 39g
- Protein: 3g
- Fiber: 0 g

Index

Conclusion

Thank you again for downloading this book!

I hope you enjoyed reading about my book!

If you enjoyed this book, please take the time to share your thoughts and post a review on Amazon. It'd be greatly appreciated!

Write me an honest review about the book – I truly value your opinion and thoughts and I will incorporate them into my next book, which is already underway.

Thank you!

If you have any questions, **feel free to contact at:** *chefhenryfox@gmail.com*

Henry Fox
www.TheCookingMAP.com/Henry-Fox

Printed in Great Britain
by Amazon

34987528R00079